IV EUROPEAN SYMPOSIUM FOR TEACHERS OF MEDIEVAL ARCHAELOGY

IV EUROPEAN SYMPOSIUM FOR TEACHERS OF MEDIEVAL ARCHAELOGY

SEVILLA-CÓRDOBA
29TH SEPTEMBER-2ND OCTOBER
1999

Editors

Magdalena Valor and Mª Antonia Carmona

JUNTA DE ANDALUCIA
CONSEJERÍA DE EDUCACIÓN Y CIENCIA

UNIVERSIDAD de SEVILLA

UNIVERSIDAD D CORDOBA

ARCHAELOGIA MEDIAEVALIS

SEVILLA, 2001

Serie: Colección Abierta
Núm.: 54

Motivo de cubierta: Ventana del Alminar de la Mezquita Mayor de Córdoba. Motivo del Cartel del Simposio.

Porvenir, 27 - 41013 Sevilla
Tlfs.: 954 487 447 - 954 487 452; Fax: 954 487 443
Correo electrónico: secpub2@pop.us.es
http://publius.cica.es

Impreso en España - Printed in Spain
I.S.B.N.: 84-472-0685-8
Depósito Legal: M-30.039-2001
Imprime: Pedro Cid, S. A.

Secretaria

D.ª MAGDALENA VALOR PIECHOTTA

Coordinación

D.ª MARÍA ANTONIA CARMONA RUIZ
D. RICARDO CÓRDOBA DE LA LLAVE

Colaboran

JUNTA DE ANDALUCÍA
Consejería de Educación y Ciencia

VICERRECTORADO DE RELACIONES INSTITUCIONALES
Y EXTENSIÓN UNIVERSITARIA
Universidad de Sevilla

VICERRECTORADO DE INVESTIGACIÓN
Universidad de Córdoba

FACULTAD DE GEOGRAFÍA E HISTORIA DE SEVILLA

FACULTAD DE FILOSOFÍA Y LETRAS DE CÓRDOBA

ARCHAEOLOGIA MEDIAEVALIS
Asociación para el Estudio y la Promoción
de la Arqueología Histórica

PREFACE

Medieval Archaeology is a discipline which has been increasingly developed in the international scientific community in recent years. The most important congresses have been:

– *Medieval Europe 1992* in York (England)

– *Medieval Europe 1997* in Bruges (Belgium)

These international conferences produced interesting pre-printed papers where we can have contacts with many research projects taking place in diverse European countries. Contributors are working in Museums, Universities, Administration, etc. and at the same time are involved in projects concerning varied topics.

We must mention here another more specialized kind of international meeting, like the very well-known *Château Gaillard* with the oldest tradition; and the much more recent *Ruralia,* now with their third proceedings published, as well as many other meetings not specifically centred around the Middle Ages.

The main aim of these meetings is the exchange of knowledge, the progress of our discipline, and personal contact with researchers from the whole of Europe.

In the same direction and with similar proposals Teachers of Medieval Archaeology have been organizing symposia since 1990, as an idea of Prof. Hans Andersson from Lund University (Sweden).

In this book, we collected many articles written by participants in the last symposium, which took place in Séville (29th September-2nd October, 1999). The lectures were organized in four sections, namely:

1) University learning in Medieval Archaeology.

2) General Questions in Current Research.

3) Specific Research Projects.

4) Medieval Archaeology in the Iberian Peninsula.

Thirteen articles are included in this book giving a short overview about significant aspects of our discipline, and ranging from the North (Norway) to the South (Spain), and from the East (Poland) to the West (Iberian Peninsula).

I like to express my gratitude for the collaboration of the Junta de Andalucía –Consejería de Educación y Ciencia–, The University of Seville, The Geography and History Faculty of Seville, the University of Cordoba and the Philosophy Faculty of Cordoba. They all made this event possible , with the result of a reinforcement of this work group and the birth of various future projects in common. Finally, since 1999, we have began to work together, with exchange between teachers and students, organisation of research projects and publications. It has taken many years ro establish a concrete starting point, if we are aware of this we will enjoy a promising future together.

MAGDALENA VALOR
University of Seville

I

University Learning in Medieval Archaelogy

TEACHING MEDIEVAL ARCHAEOLOGY ON INTERNET. EXPERIENCES FROM LUND UNIVERSITY

Hans Andersson
Lund University, Sweden

DISTANCE LEARNING OR DISTRIBUTED LEARNING

Distance learning or to use an another word *distributed learning* is not a new idea. From my youth l remember of the correspondence schools which were very active in distributing courses of varying size on very different themes. Quite, early on, many courses, especially in languages, were taught on the radio. And from the 60's television has played a great role. In many countries this has been an important part of education policy. Today the rise of the Internet has meant a new situation, and we now have a new instrument for *distance learning or distributed learning.* If you look around on the Internet you can find many different courses, including some at university level. There are also virtual universities, which only exist in cyberspace where you can get degrees of different kinds.

There are now many regular universities which are engaged in this kind of training (for example University of California Extension online http://www. Berkeley.edu). My example is from medieval archaeology in Lund. I will talk about our experiences: what has been successful and what has been problematic. The main reason why I give this presentation is that l believe that this way of working could be a way to cooperate and create broader possibilities for teaching in a relatively small discipline like ours, medieval archaeology.

I will use our beginners' course in medieval archaeology as an example. We have given the course on the Internet twice. We are now discussing how to continue, what changes we must make and what new forms we have to find. But first some words about the university framework in Lund for this course.

GENERAL STRATEGY

Lund University has decided to gather all virtual educational resources in Lund Virtual University (http://www.tov.lu.se/distansutbildning). The university will support measures in the realisation of interactive net-based distance education. Distance education should be decentralized within the university. A teacher must be able to carry out on campus courses as well as distance courses. Today there are about 150 web-based distance courses –developed and under development at Lund University in different disciplines, among them quite a few within the arts and humanities.

To reach the goals the following specifications for a web-based, integrated tool for distributed courses have been formulated.

- easy to use for teachers and students
- platform independent (Win & Mac & Unix)
- at the cutting edge of technology
- built of standard components (exchangeable)
- allowing high interactivity-communication
- easy to develop further (pedagogy, etc.)

As a part of the implemetation of The Lund Model the interactive distance learning tool LUVIT has been developed (http://www.luvit.com). It gives the teachers the **opportunity to** create courses through the web and interactively communicate with the students. Within the LUVIT framework there are several tools for creating and publishing web courses. The major features are:

- Course creation tool
- Web, publishing tool
- Multiple communication modes
- Student progress- and access-statistics, auto-corrected tests and self evaluations
- Access control and guest accounts. Navigation tool
- Course calendar
- Direct links to the University Library resources and databases
- Effective search methods

These tools mean that the teacher has easy access to web publishing, can check the individual learning processes, can choose when and where to work more freely and communicate in several ways. LUVIT also gives the students individual responsibility.

MEDIEVAL ARCHAEOLOGY AND LUVIT

The course which we have transformed into a web course is for beginners. It comprises 20 weeks and is a full-time course. It is divided in three parts:

- introduction
- countryside and town
- church and castle

The students have a reading course with books and papers (in Scandinavian languages and English). For examination they summarise their readings in short essays. The teacher formulates the problems to be solved.

In the LUVIT framework we have presented introductions to the courses, also longer texts as substitute for oral lectures with illustration material. We have formulated problems to be solved during the reading, and we have given the students other exercises to do, for example to visit a medieval monument in their vicinity and make a description of it.

We have combined this with lists of literature they should read. They have also got links to medieval material that is available on the net (quite a lot). Naturally we has also published schedules and the like.

Interactivity is of course a central question. The teacher can reach everybody with general messages during the course, but even more important is that the teacher can communicate individually with every student and of course vice versa. There are also chat possibilities between the students and between teachers and students. It is also possible to form smaller groups with communication only within the groups. The texts which are produced by the students are also published on LUVIT. It is a basic pedagogical idea behind the LUVIT conception that everybody should have the chance to read each other's texts.

MEDIEVAL ARCHAEOLOGY AND LUVIT. SOME EXPERIENCES

One must realise that this is a special form of teaching. You don't have the usual direct contact with the students, eye to eye. But the fact that you have to communicate with the students through the net creates another form of contact that can at best be quite rewarding for the teaching and learning. But the replies must be rather quick. There must be something which exerts pressure on or urges on the students.

The students get training in writing, which is very good.

I think that those students who are the most motivated and independent achieve the best results in this type of course. Not everybody is fully aware that a course like this, which they follow at home, is just as hard as a course followed at the university. One of my Internet student said to me that I must realise that she also had a full-time job.

We had a fair amount of technical difficulties at the beginning. When we started, the LUVIT system was quite new and there was too much optimism that it would function flawlessly from the beginning. So there was a lot of frustration both for the teachers and for the students. But it has became much better now, even if there still are and will be problems. There are so many things which must function and function together. For example the student PCs must perform adequately, otherwise it can be difficult to access the material in LUVIT.

For our own part we will change from full-time courses to part-time. We must also change and modernise our basic material. We started relatively simply, but now we especially have to develop our illustration material. We must also discuss making textbooks, which we can publish. In theory it should be possible to publish other texts on the Internet, but there are still complicated copyright problems to be solved.

THE FUTURE

We may have different opinions on the use of information technology. There are, especially among the humanities, those who have a rather negative attitude to IT. And I understand this hesitation because there has not been so very much material until rather recently. Many emphasize also that personal contact is a very important thing. Is it possible to get it on the Internet?

On the other hand the development just now is very rapid. It is possible that many of our students will sign up to some course given on the Internet, coming from anywhere in the world, besides the courses they take at our departments. They will combine courses from different universities for their university degree.

In this perspective we must look on IT as a great opportunity especially for us who represent a discipline which is quite small in a university perspective. But to get the best strength we have to cooperate. Besides our often national perspective we could give our students the chance to get introductory courses, for example, in Spanish medieval archaeology or in German or in Polish, etc. The theory in Medieval Archaeology could be taught from very different points of view. We could coordinate specialist courses, also on doctoral level.

We all have a lot to do, but we have to collaborate for the future to make medieval archaeology stronger. But not just that. We have to collaborate to be aware that medieval archaeology is not a national project but has a wider scope, something which must be mirrored in our teaching and research.

So let us discuss these questions quite practically.

- Can we find ways to plan such work together?
- Who, for example, is interested in working with us in Lund to develop course material? Shall we apply for money together? Are their any chances to get EU-money for this?
- Can we plan for joint courses?

- Can we produce course material together? It is very expensive for our small departments to make really professional material. Is it possible to co-operate?
- Could it be possible to publish collections of material and reports of excavations, and other data on the Intemet or on a CD-ROM?
- We can set up a joint homepage on medieval archaeology. We can try to do such a site in Lund, where we can gather material about what is going on, with all these links to other departments of medieval archaeology. This idea is not new, but now there are simple technical solutions, which can be handled by everyone.

When we started the ESTMA conferences we had the idea that they should end with better and deeper cooperation. In a way it has been better, but when we come to the teaching on the ground level very little has happened in this respect I hope that there still are possibilities to promote a deeper understanding for the necessity of working together not only in research but also in teaching for us medieval archaeologists.

THE ENGLISH TEXT REVISED BY ALAN CROZIER

TEACHING EUROPEAN MEDIEVAL ARCHAEOLOGY. THE PROBLEM OF TEXTBOOKS

Else Roesdahl
Aarhus University, Denmark

We need a European –wide textbook of medieval archaeology– a student textbook reviewing important European aspects of medieval archaeology and taking a European overview, not one that is merely local or regional.

I deliberately raise this problem in this forum of university teachers in the subject. The production of a European textbook would seem a natural outcome of these meetings, especially if they are to continue. The process of achieving such a book would add value to the meetings (and our teaching), and the purposes of the meetings would become more obvious than they are at present. More important, a textbook –or textbooks– of medieval European archaeology would up-date our subject in relation to current world-views and to the current situation in Europe.

Medieval archaeology is relatively new as a university discipline if compared with many other academic subjects including prehistoric archaeology. Our departments are organised and staffed in many different ways. Our chronological frameworks vary considerably, especially in our conception of the beginning of the medieval period. Teaching normally focuses on the region in which we live and work –in Denmark, for example, we focus on South Scandinavia and North Germany. On the other hand, we all probably have courses in European medieval archaeology and invite guest lecturers to contribute to our understanding of other countries or regions. Many of us take our students abroad to look at the archaeology of other countries and regions. Some of us run joint research projects with colleagues in other countries. We probably all try hard to relate the European background of our discipline to local features and developments, and try to give our students a European outlook –they badly need it in order to get some understanding of what medieval culture is.

There was a time when we needed textbooks on many subjects, including surveys of the medieval archaeology of our own regions. There is indeed still much to do in this field –many countries and regions still need their own textbook. But we have come some way in the last fifteen years. We have seen, among other books, Helen Clarke's *The Archaeology of Medieval England,* 1984; Terry Barry's *The Archaeology of Medieval Ireland,* 1987; Günther Fehring's *Einführung in die Archäologie des Mittelalters,* 1987 (English ed., *The Archaeology of Medieval Germany – an introduction,* 1991); Knud Liebgott's *Dansk Middelalderarkæologi* (Danish Medieval Archaeology), 1989; Leszek Kajzer's *Wstep do Archeologii Historycznej w Polsce,* 1996 (with summary in English, 'The Introduction to the Historical Archaeology in Poland'); not to mention the book I edited in 1999, *Dagligliv i Danmarks Middelalder –en arkæologisk kulturhistorie* (Daily Life in Medieval Denmark– an archaeological cultural history), which encompassed the work of twelve specialists.

It is of course much easier to synthesise the archaeology of a small country like Denmark than to write on the medieval archaeology on the whole of all vast and varied Europe. But we urgently need such synthesis. It will not be easy, but it can be done if properly organised. We must have experienced editors, reliable authors, efficient arrangements for the supply of illustrations and a good publisher –all based on tough planning, serious deadlines and good funding.

I do not think it possible for a single author to write such a book. Our subject has grown enormously during the last decades and outgrown such a possibility –nowadays it is hardly possible for one author to cover one country in a near-comprehensive way. The days of great European textbooks by one author are gone, despite the obvious qualities of one-author-books. Stuart Piggott's *Ancient Europe,* 1965, splendidly surveyed aspects of the archaeology of this part of the world right from the beginning until about the Birth of Christ and is still used in university teaching in prehistoric archaeology, at least in my country.

Synthetic books on Vikings, however, such as James Graham-Campbell (ed.): *Cultural Atlas of the Viking World,* 1994, might help define a model. It covers some three hundred years and a wide geographical area –Vikings ventured far: from Scandinavia to North Atlantic lands and America, and to the lands south and east of the Baltic, to Russia, the British Isles, the coastal parts of the Continent including France, and even to Seville. The book is mainly archaeological in approach, but there are also contributions on important subjects other than archaeology, among them runes and religion, and the topics treated are all seen in an historical context. Graham-Campbell edited the book and also wrote some of it; there were altogether five authors. It is well illustrated with good quality photographs, drawings and reconstructions, all in colour. Many copies were published. A book on the archaeology of medieval Scandinavia, which some of us planned about fifteen years ago but which never materialised, was to have had about eight authors and two or three editors.

I would like to lay before you my preliminary thoughts on how an 'Archaeology of Medieval Europe' might be organised. First, the actual contents should be discussed in detail in a working group. Second, I would suggest that it should be published in two volumes (in English), each about 330 pages. The first volume could cover the period 1000-1350; the second, 1350-1550. The area conceived as Europe must be defined, but the whole area would not be treated equally in all chapters or in both volumes. Each volume should have about ten chapters, each written by one or two authors, and the topics treated would not be parallel in the volumes. Rather, the chapters would investigate a series of important topics which would illuminate overall problems such, for example, as regionalism as opposed to common European cultural features; the meeting and interaction of cultures; tradition and innovation; infrastructure; the archaeology of devotion; aspects of technology; food and its production; non-agrarian production; houses and how they were lived in; economic systems; decorative arts, and so on. There would be foot/endnotes or an extensive annotated bibliography for each chapter.

An editorial board should be formed consisting of a maximum five experienced academics from different parts of Europe. They would take responsibility for the project, secure the overall coherence and balance between the volumes, and advise and assist the editors (one or two for each volume), the picture editors and the authors. There should be formal contracts with all involved. ESTMA meetings might be used as a medium for discussion. One or two specially designed symposia could be arranged during the working process. They should also make suggestions as to funding and subvention.

The textbooks should mainly target university students in medieval archaeology, but they should also be of interest to other medievalists and to an interested lay audience. They should, therefore, be written in good and fluent language without unnecessary jargon, and an experienced academic 'language cleaner'/translator must be associated with the project. The volumes must be well illustrated, partly in colour, and the illustrations and captions must be edited with as much care as the text.

Serious funding would be needed, but being a European project it might not be too difficult to obtain. There could be expenses for editors for realistic work periods. Translations (or corrections of texts) must be paid and will not be cheap. The production of illustrations and copyright fees must be taken into account, although ESTMA members might agree to provide illustrations, for which they or their departments hold the copyright, free of charge; and they might be able to arrange free use of other illustrations. Some travelling costs for editors and some of the authors must be met; symposia must be funded.

There is no doubt that the realisation of such a project is quite complicated and will be time-consuming for all involved. If, however, the idea is considered to be worth while, I would suggest that a planning committee be set up during this congress. There will still be a long way to go.

POSTSCRIPT

The discussion following the lecture revealed general enthusiasm for the idea. There were, however, arguments in favour of three instead of two volumes, the first to cover the period c. 400-950. Web publishing was also discussed. Various definitions of Europe were suggested; one was that it should comprise the area where Romanesque and Gothic art was adopted. Another suggested area could comprise that area which became Roman Catholic Europe –the area where Latin was the common language and where Rome was concieved as central.

An interim planning group was organised consisting of eight or nine members working on different geographical parts of what became Roman Catholic Europe. Johnny De Meulemeester agreed to be convener of a meeting in Brussels in spring 2000. The meeting would produce outline suggestions for the contents and production of what would probably be three volumes. It would encompass suggestions for topics, authors, editors and organisation (including a timetable). It should also make proposals as to funding and publishing, and should be ready for presentation and discussion at the next ESTMA meeting at Bamberg in the autumn of 2001.

RESEARCH AND TEACHING IN EXPERIMENTAL MEDIAEVAL ARCHAEOLOGY. L'ESQUERDA, A PROJECT ABOUT AGRICULTURE, TOOLS AND CONSTRUCTION IN MEDIAEVAL AGES*

Imma Ollich i Castanyer
University of Barcelona

The archaeological excavations in the Iberian and mediaeval site of L'Esquerda began in 1977, carried on by a team of the University of Barcelona. This ancient iberian "oppidum" and mediaeval deserted village is placed by 70 km north of Barcelona. The discovery of a granary, dated between half-end 13th century a.D. and identified by paleocarpologycal analysis, was the beginning of a new line of research about mediaeval agriculture and experimental archaeology.

Since 1991 the mediaeval site of L'Esquerda is the place where is developed the LEAF Project on Experimental Archaeology, approved by the Ministerio de Educación y Cultura (DGICYT PB90-0430, PB94-0842 & PB98-1241). A land next to the site has been arranged to make some experimental fields, where each year different cereals are grown, in order to study the process of mediaeval agriculture and its productivity. We carry on also experiments on construction, reproducing the granary itself. All of these research activities are made with students of the University of Barcelona, who come to the site not only to dig up, but to take part in special courses about experimental mediaeval archaeology: practices with Mediaeval Archaeology students, Master and Doctor students, Summer University Courses, and other. So, the site of L'Esquerda is a place to research but also for teaching mediaeval archaeology.

I. THE SITE

The iberian and mediaeval site of L'Esquerda is next to the village of Roda de Ter, 70 km northwards Barcelona, just placed on a meander of the river Ter. The landscape is made by an eocenic plateau, called Plana de Vic, surrounded

* I would like to thank specially my colleague Montserrat de Rocafiguera, co-director of the archaeological excavations at the site of L'Esquerda, for her help and her comments to this paper

everywhere by mountains. From the Pyrenean mountains, where it springs up, the river crosses this plateau in its north-side, before leaving the region in its way to the Mediterranean coast.

The settlement is placed at the top of a meander that forms a peninsula of 12 ha, only accesible by the North. The highest part near the romanesque church is occupated by the mediaeval site. A big fortification is implanted in the north side, where the sedimentary accumulation has preserved the iberian and prehistoric sediments. The archaeological excavations give us a large chronological sequence, from the later Bronze Age (8th century b.C.) to 14th century a.D. (OLLICH-ROCAFIGUERA, 1992).

II. THE RESEARCH

Since 1977, the site is digged out annually by a team of the University of Barcelona. The students of mediaeval archaeology can work and practice field archaeology digging directly on a mediaeval deserted village. For a season of a fortnight, the University of Barcelona convalides a maximum of 3 credits in the student's History studies.

Really, the research process itself and its management brought us to create three things: 1) a little Museum in the town of Roda de Ter; 2) a Laboratory near the site where to work and study the archaeological artifacts from the site; and 3) the Experimental Fields, where to carry on the trials about experimental archaeology. So we must distinguish between the direct research at the site, and research using experimental archaeology in an special area.

– The research at the site

They are the real archaeological excavations, where come some students each summer and work at the site. They learn not only the field work, but how to arrange an excavation, technics and record systems, data-base, cleaning and drawing pieces of pottery, and how to classify them. Mostly of the students have studied the matter "Mediaeval Archaeology" at the Faculty. But the real problems are on the field.

During the year, the students who are interested can come to the Laboratory one day a week to work and learn more about the archaeological pieces. So this Workroom-Laboratory, placed near the site and provided by the town of Roda de Ter, is very helpful to analyse, to restore and to catalogue.

– Experimental archaeology (LEAF project)

During the excavations made between 1986 and 1988, in the mediaeval deserted village was found an structure that had been burned full of seeds in middle or last 13th Century. The analyses made on these seeds identified the structure as a granary. It was constructed like the rest of the houses of the mediaeval town, made with stone and adobe. The structure was a 5×5 m square, with

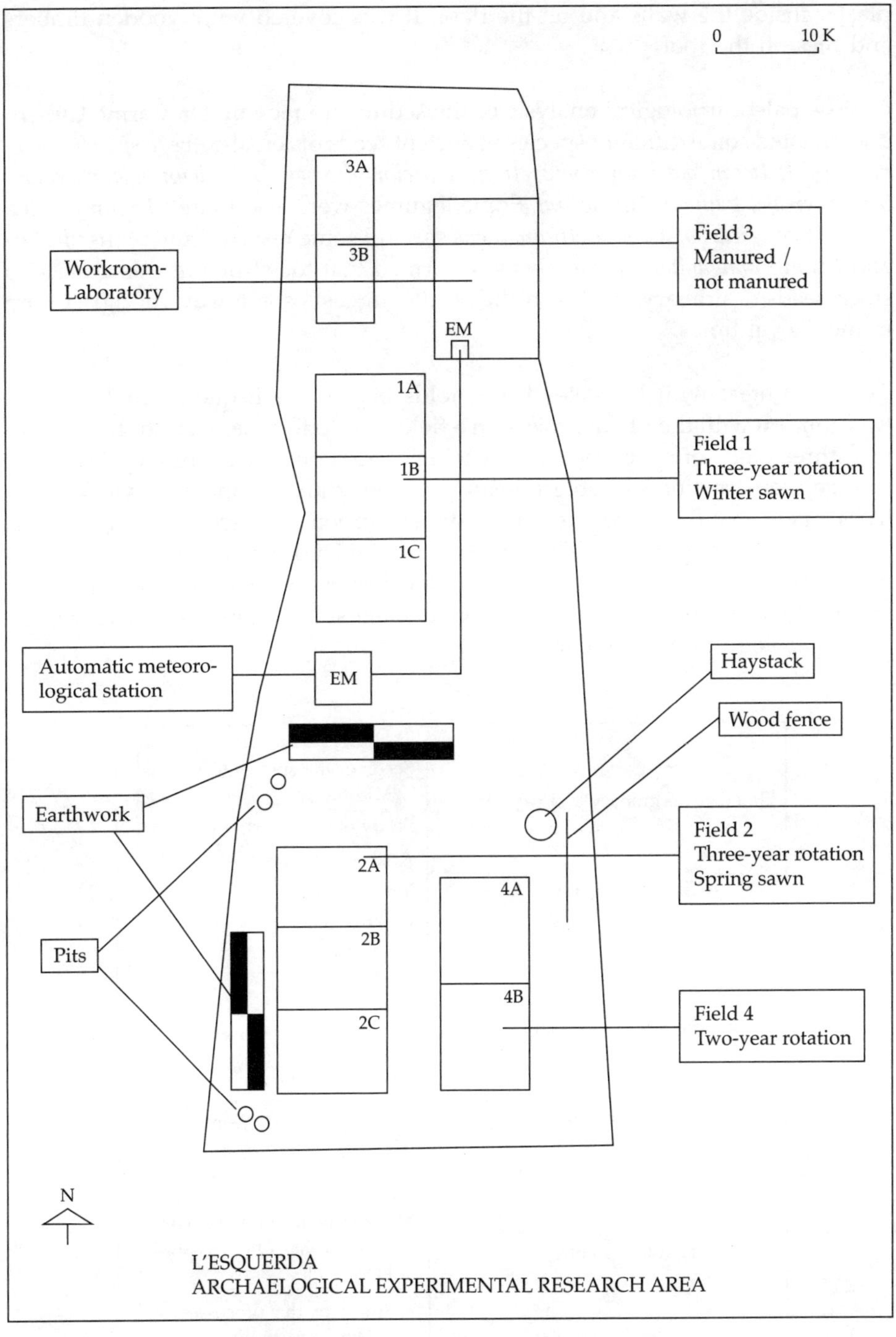

Fig. 1. L'Esquerda archaeological experimental research area.

plaster inside the walls and on the floor. It was covered with wooden timbers and tiles on the roof.

The paleocarpological analysis of the sediment made by Dr. Carme Cubero documented some different species of ancient seeds of cereals: *Avena sp., Hordeum vulgare, Triticum aestivum-compactum, Triticum dicoccum, Triticum monococcum, Secale cereale, Panicum miliaceum.* Some legumes were also found: *Ervum ervilia, Vicia sativa, Vicia sp., Cicer aretinum, Lens sp.;* and some rests of fruits: *Vitis vinifera* and *Prunus amigdalus.* This analysis confirmed that the structure was a place to stock seeds, a granary. And also the study suggests some ways of agriculture in mediaeval times.

The contact with Dr. Peter J. Reynolds began at L'Esquerda in 1990, and was gone on with the LEAF Project. In a field next to the site, around the Laboratory, three kinds of experiments are beeing carried on: agricultural cycles, grain storage (construction of subterranean pits and granary) and earthworks. The trials made in l'Esquerda are based directly upon the research programmes pioneered at Butser Ancient Farm in England by Dr. Reynolds. He is a member of the research's team of L'Esquerda, and as Professor Visitor of the University of Barcelona he comes every year to give some special courses on experimental archaeology to the students.

(mediaeval granary and carpology) ↓ AGRICULTURAL CYCLES	Seeds of the species tested in Middle Ages Study of the growing process Analysis of weeds Yield study Ethnoarchaeological study
(mediaeval granary and pits) ↓ STORAGE	PITS: • building • use GRANARY: • building • use
(Stratigraphy) ↓ EARTHWORK	• Construction of two ditches and banks, and a wood fence • Study of the processes of erosion and sedimentation • Study of weed colonization

Fig. 2. The LEAF project.

III. TEACHING MEDIAEVAL ARCHAEOLOGY

Actually the students of History at the University of Barcelona can study Mediaeval Archaeology as a subject of 6 credits offered by the Department of Mediaeval History. Even, during their second cycle (3rd and 4th year), they can choose between different subjects, all referred to mediaeval archaeology: mediaeval technology, ceramics and other artifacts. People that want to complete their theoretical learning must assist to some of the summer excavations organized and directed by the Department: they can choose between the castles of Mataplana and Mur (11th-12th centuries); the mediaeval deserted villages of l'Esquerda and València d'Àneu; the pottery kilns of Cabrera d'Anoia; or the iron forge of La Fabregada. Most of these sites are placed in the Pyrenean mountains or near of them. Digging up during two weeks in summer is 3 credits. The student is included with the archaeological team, and so he/she can learn directly at the site.

Field archaeology doesn't stop after summer. During the academic course, the student can continue the work in the laboratory at University: to classify and drawing pieces of pottery, bones, iron and other materials; to participate in all the study of the excavation and to prepare for publication.

The students wanted and asked for this speciality for a long time, because the studies in Archaeology finished in late roman and paleocristian times. During a lot of years only one matter on medieval archaeology was included in the studies for Ph.D. degree.

The first Master in Mediaeval Archaeology by the University of Barcelona was organised in 1989-1990, and 25 people that had finished their history studies followed the two-years courses. Most of them were interested in learning but also in working in mediaeval archaeology. The lessons were both theoretical and practical, and included such different subjects as Phisical Antropology, Data Base and Computer Register, Archaeological Drawing, Sediment Analysis... and many others. All the practices were done directly at the mediaeval deserted village of L'Esquerda, using the site as a teaching-room.

This site is also used generally during the summer courses of the University of Vic: since 1997, the "Universitat d'Estiu de Vic" has offered an special course on Experimental Archaeology, as long as a week in July. Teachers and students work together directly at the site, the laboratory and fields of L'Esquerda, using all the place as an open air laboratory. The courses are on experimental mediaeval agriculture and construction, and the students can practice directly with the harvest and storage. They can cut the cereal ears by hand, or with a billhook, like in mediaeval times; then they must to separate the wheat from the straw, that is stocked outside in a haystack. The harvest is carried into the laboratory to weigh the production, and to count and measure the ears. After, the spikes will be stock in the granary or in the subterranean pits.

In the courses done about construction, the students learned and collaborated in making the mediaeval granary, real size, as that it was found in the site: making the walls of stone and adobe, and the roof, with wood timbers and mediaeval tiles.

Our experience about such a learning, direct on the site and practices on experimental archaeology is really good. The students like so much this kind of learning and are very interested in continue making real things and experiences, that complete their theoretical studies. So, we think that work together research and teaching is a good way to carry on with the studies of Mediaeval Archaeology at the University. For the next course, the University of Barcelona has included a new matter: Mediaeval Field Archaelogy, that will be given at the site of l'Esquerda in 2002.

BIBLIOGRAPHY

OCAÑA, M. (1998): *El món agrari i els cicles agrícoles a la Catalunya Vella (s. IX-XIII),* tesi de Llicenciatura 1994, Universitat de Barcelona, Departament d'Història Medieval, col. *Documenta,* 1, Barcelona, 136 pp.

OLLICH, I., CUBERO, C. (1989): "Paleocarpologia i agricultura a l'Edat Mitjana: l'excavació i estudi d'un graner medieval a Catalunya", a *III Congreso de Arqueología Medieval Española,* Oviedo, març 1989, Actes Comunicacions, pp. 73-85.

OLLICH, I. (1990): "L'ús d'un jaciment com a camp docent i experimental. Master d'Arqueologia Medieval: Necròpolis i ritual funerari", a *V Jornades d'Arqueologia Medieval a Catalunya,* Universitat de Barcelona, juny 1990, pp. 49-53.

OLLICH, I., CUBERO, C. (1990): "El graner de l'Esquerda: un conjunt tecnològic agrari a la Catalunya Medieval", a *La vida medieval a les dues vessants del Pirineu (1r i 2n curs d'Arqueologia d'Andorra),* Andorra, pp. 33-47.

OLLICH, I., ROCAFIGUERA, M. (1992): "Ancient patterns of settlement and urbanism: the mediaeval site of l'Esquerda (Catalonia)", *Mediaeval Europe 1992. An International Conference,* University of York, pre-printed papers, vol. 8: Rural Settlement, pp. 131-137.

OLLICH, I., ROCAFIGUERA, M. (1993): "Antiguas pautas de asentamiento y urbanismo en el yacimiento medieval de L'Esquerda (Catalunya)", a *Boletín de Arqueología Medieval,* 7, Madrid, pp. 11-20.

OLLICH, I., REYNOLDS, P.J., ROCAFIGUERA, M. (1993): "*L'Earthwork* de l'Esquerda. Un experiment en processos de formació", a *IV Congreso de Arqueología Espacial (Procesos Postdeposicionales),* Teruel, Colegio Universitario de Teruel, pp. 341-352.

OLLICH, I., REYNOLDS, P.J., ROCAFIGUERA, M. (1994): "Agricultura medieval i arqueologia experimental: el projecte de l'Esquerda", a *IV Congrés d'Arqueologia Medieval Espanyola,* Alacant 1993, tom. III, pp. 701-709.

OLLICH, I., ROCAFIGUERA, M. (1994): *L'oppidum ibèric de l'Esquerda (Roda de Ter, Osona),* Departament de Cultura, Generalitat de Catalunya, Col.lecció Memòries d'Excavacions Arqueològiques, nº 7, Barcelona, 99 pp.

OLLICH, I., OCAÑA, M., RAMISA, M., ROCAFIGUERA, M. (1995): *A banda i banda del Ter, Història de Roda,* Ajuntament de Roda de Ter / Eumo Editorial (L'Entorn, 30), 279 pp.

OLLICH, I., REYNOLDS, P.J., OCAÑA, M., ROCAFIGUERA, M. (1996): "Experimentació arqueològica sobre sistemes de conreu medievals. Primers resultats del projecte de l'Esquerda", a *XIV Jornades d'Estudis Històrics Locals: La Mediterrània, àrea de convergència de sistemes alimentaris (segles v-xviii)*, Institut d'Estudis Baleàrics, Palma de Mallorca, pp. 153-168.

OLLICH, I., REYNOLDS, P.J., ROCAFIGUERA, M., OCAÑA, M. (1997): "L'Esquerda. Ecology, environment and agricultural productivity", *Mediaeval Europe 1997. An International Conference*, Brugge (pre-printed papers).

OLLICH, I., ROCAFIGUERA, M. (1998): "L'Esquerda. Un projecte de recerca arqueològica a Osona", a *Memòria del Congrés de Cultura d'Osona*, Vic, gener 1997, pp. 278-281.

OLLICH, I. (Coord.), BLANCAFORT, F., CABALLÉ, A., COSTA, R., ESPONA, P., MARTÍ, J., OCAÑA, M., REYNOLDS, P.J., RINCÓN, M.A., RIU, M., ROCAFIGUERA, M., SERRAT, D. (1998): *Experimentació arqueològica sobre conreus medievals a l'Esquerda, 1991-1994. Arqueologia experimental: aplicació a l'agricultura medieval mediterrània (DGICYT PB90-0430)*, Universitat de Barcelona, Departament d'Història Medieval, Col. Monografies d'Arqueologia Medieval i Post-medieval, 3, Barcelona, 253 pp.

REYNOLDS, P.J. (1988): *Arqueologia Experimental. Una perspectiva de futur*, Eumo Ed., Vic, 229 pp.

REYNOLDS, P.J. (1997): "Mediaeval Cereal Yields in Catalonia and England: An empirical challenge", a *ACTA Historica et Archaeologica MEDIAEVALIA*, 18, Universitat de Barcelona, pp. 495-507.

II

General Questions In Present Research

RECENT DEVELOPMENTS AND NEW APPROACHES TO THE ARCHAEOLOGY OF MEDIEVAL GREECE

John Bintliff
University of Leiden, Netherlands

INTRODUCTION

Medieval archaeology in Greece has till recently been dominated by the study of Byzantine churches, icons, and castles. A new wave of information, however, is coming out of two parallel developments. Firstly, a renewed interest in post-Roman excavated deposits can be observed, especially those encountered in major urban excavations (and most notably at the key Frankish centre of Corinth). Secondly –and much more widespread– there is the striking evidence for Medieval rural life that is coming from a series of regional surface surveys inaugurated over the last twenty years and now emerging in final publications.

The archaeology of town and country which is now maturing is not confined to the chronology and typology of Greek medieval culture, but includes innovative work in relating chronicles and tax cadasters to rural settlement systems discovered through intensive fieldwork, and the study of ethnicity and popular lifestyles from the material culture record.

This paper will review these developments and illustrate them by reference to a series of recent and ongoing archaeological projects in Greece, and in particular from my own project in Boeotia, Central Greece.

TRADITIONAL WORK ON MEDIEVAL GREEK ARCHAEOLOGY AND RECENT WORK ON THE MONUMENTS

Medieval Greece has been richly served by research and publications throughout the 20th century, focussing on the highpoints of Medieval art and architecture –the churches, monasteries and their icons (notably the work of Orlandos) and the major castles (especially the work of Bon), accompanied by a rich number of studies of the chronicles and archives (Miller, Setton). In the first half of this century an unavoidable side-result of largescale American excavations planned to uncover major Classical monuments in the ancient centre (agora) at Athens and in that of Corinth, was the revealing of significant Medieval levels.

Much to their credit, the excavation directors commissioned pioneering studies of the finds (e.g. Frantz [1942] for the Agora), the most substantial of which –Morgan (1942 for Corinth) remains a major sourcebook for the modern study of Byzantine and Frankish ceramics in the Aegean.

A recent project by the Austrian Academy of Sciences, the *Tabula Byzantina,* has been issuing regular volumes of an atlas of the Byzantine empire, province by province, under the general direction of Professor Johannes Koder (the first volume, *Hellas und Thessalia,* 1976, being especially useful for my own research in Central Greece). Alongside excellent maps showing the location of monuments, excavations and literary topographic references, the texts of these volumes offer historical resumes and discussions for each Byzantine province (or *theme)* under a number of headings, and in general this series provides an ideal and relatively up-to-date review of the published evidence for Medieval monuments and the localities mentioned in the sources.

An example of more recent work on the medieval monuments is the examination by Peter Lock of the freestanding towers of South-Central Greece (Lock, 1986, 1996), which are probably to be dated for the majority to the Frankish period (13th to 15th centuries a.D.). Lock combines careful modern architectural survey with pioneering discussion of the social, and especially feudal contexts in which these towers may have functioned. A much more recent monumental landscape is represented by similar pioneer work by Todd Whitelaw on the rural structures of the island of Kea (1991, in Davies et al.), interrelated complexes of terrace and other field walls, paths and isolated farmhouses of the 19th century a.D. Once again a painstaking survey of large areas of these features is accompanied by a highly insightful discussion of the socioeconomic circumstances within which this landscape was created. Equally fascinating is the careful documentation and mapping of Post-Medieval khans (wayside hostels) in the rugged uplands of Aetolia province in Central Greece as part of the long-running Dutch Aetolia Project (Bommeljé and Doorn, 1996) in relation to historical geographical analysis of communication systems in the long-term within that region.

This last example introduces the fruitful combination of oral, archival and standing building evidence to reconstruct a series of post-Classical structures. There are indeed examples where no physical trace remains of even outstanding medieval and post-medieval monuments. One such example came to my notice at an exhibition of photographs of ecclesiastical art and architecture in the Central Greek province of Boeotia by a friend –George Kopanyas, in the regional capital of Livadhia. In the background of a splendid icon of St. John the Baptist from Thebes I observed what appeared to be a detailed representation of that town at the height of the Ottoman era, including a mosque of remarkable proportions and complexity. Fortunately our Project Ottoman archivist, Professor Michael Kiel, was also a specialist in architecture, and has recently published this lost monument (Kiel, 1999), based entirely on this image, attributing to it a date in the early 17th century and classing it as a major provincial imitation of the great mosques of Istanbul.

ARCHAEOLOGICAL FIELD SURVEY

Since the 1960s in Greece, regional field survey has been a major research tool for understanding the development of settlement, population and land-use in the long-term. However, even when methods moved from the more superficial, extensive survey to the slower, field-by-field, intensive approach, the recognition and study of post-classical sites has been limited. One difficulty has been the absence of detailed ceramic sequences for worn surface ceramics and the great shortage of specialists with knowledge of such material. Since the pioneer urban publications from Corinth and Athens only a few case-studies have provided textbook examples to compare surface ceramics with (the finest by far being John Hayes' modern classic –the Saraçhane Excavation report [Hayes, 1992]); one can also mention the growing series of studies by Guy Sanders on the older and recent medieval excavations at Corinth and for the Cyclades (Sanders, 1987, 1995, 1996), and the fine research of Papanikola-Bakirtzis into medieval glazed wares (eg 1999).

On the Boeotia Regional Survey Project, which I have jointly directed with Anthony Snodgrass of Cambridge University since 1978, we are strikingly fortunate in that the surface ceramics of post-classical date (almost entirely made within the region itself), are of excellent quality and rich variety. Primary work by John Hayes on the basic chronology is now being supplemented by Joanita Vroom (generously funded by the Leverhulme Foundation and currently by the Dutch Science Research Council), who is fine-tuning the sequence and investigating aspects such as changing dining habits through the period. The very numerous post-classical sites discovered by our field survey ensure that many are occupied in limited timespans, allowing the possibility of creating a floating chronology of ceramic types which can be given approximate chronological associations through the survey equivalent of "closed assemblages", with the help of occasional well-dated forms or imports (eg Vroom, 1997). Even from the preliminary stage, based on the basic chronology established by John Hayes, it has been possible to begin to map the evolution of rural settlement through contrasting phases of several hundred years' duration, such as Early, Middle or Late Byzantine / Early Frankish, Late Frankish to Early Turkish, and Late Turkish to Early Modern (cf. Bintliff, 1996b, Bintliff and Snodgrass, 1988).

Naturally the typical post-classical surface site is merely a concentration of potsherds in a ploughed field, occasionally with fragments of house walls, but one can occasionally come upon more substantial remains hitherto unrecorded scientifically. One such example came to light in Boeotia at the end of the 1980s, when unparalleled drought coupled with opportunistic expansion of irrigated land caused a dramatic lowering in the level of Lake Ilike. Nineteenth-century maps and reports evidenced the existence of a medieval tower of the kind published by Peter Lock, whose top emerged from the lake in very rare drought years. A visit to the location revealed not only the complete tower but a surrounding medieval estate centre, its walls washed clean by the lake and the similarly washed ceramics lying in each room and open space. We were able to make a detailed plan of the site and collect the ceramics in each architectural context, but the final publication of the Klimmataria site will take some time as its complexity outstrips any other surface survey site outside our work on Greco-Roman cities. However it very quickly became apparent that a close parallel exists between the tower and those typical Frankish feudal monuments common elsewhere in Boeotia, and moreover equally good parallels can be found for the plan of the surrounding estate complex with those being published for Frankish rural estates in the contemporary Crusader Kingdom of Jerusalem (Ellenblum et al., 1996, Ellenblum 1998).

In the remainer of this paper I shall turn to the contribution regional survey can make to fundamental historical issues for Medieval Greece, and to new approaches to the social and economic history of the period through the study of material culture. The examples given emanate from my own project in Boeotia, Central Greece.

MAJOR HISTORICAL QUESTIONS BEING ADDRESSED IN REGIONAL SURVEY

The Transition from Late Antiquity to the Early Middle Ages

Firstly it is worth reminding researchers in the West of Europe that this transitional phase belongs to the period between the 7th and 9th centuries a.D., since at least till the later 6th century, the Eastern Roman or Byzantine Empire was highly flourishing. Now one of the clearest ways to try and focus in on the nature of the changes for typical communities at the village and smaller urban level in Greece, is to start with the mature settlement network of Greco-Roman times across a large province like Boeotia, and compare this level of larger, nucleated settlements with that of the High Middle Ages (Bintliff, 1995, 1997). Since intensive field survey can only cover small sectors of such a province, we have to use extensive and topographic survey for this level of generalisation –but fortunately it is in the classes of small villages-hamlets and isolated farms that intensive survey makes the most dramatic enrichment of our map of archaeological sites, whilst the larger settlements can be reasonably located from extensive and topographic survey. Thus, if we plot settlements mentioned in the historic sources, Frankish (Crusader) feudal towers, churches, and excavated sites with evidence for the High Middle Ages (ca. 1000-1400 a.D.), it becomes apparent that a high number of Greco-Roman villages and towns are still in occupation at this later time, a fact which is a first argument for continuity of occupation –and perhaps a significant element of population continuity, across the "Dark Ages" that intervened.

On the other hand, there is a tradition of historical geography, to which I suscribe, that of the *Siedlungskammer* of the German Landeskunde school (eg Lehmann, 1939; Bintliff, 1994) recently elaborated into the *Community Area* theory of the current Prague school of landscape archaeology (Kuna, 1991), and this reminds us that diversified landscapes tend to create definite "constraints and possibilities" for settlement, often in or around certain recurrent places in the landscape (the product of physical topography, soil types, technological and land use regimes, natural paths of communication, etc.). It is therefore quite possible for apparent continuities in the placing of settlements over time to be the result of convergence of natural conditions, or ways of using the landscape, rather than due to genuine continuities of local peoples.

To help resolve the balance between these contrasted processes we need more precise information, and as noted above, this is an area where intensive survey of small districts at the *Siedlungskammer-Community Area* scale, combined with historical and archival evidence, can provide major insights. In the Valley of the Muses in Boeotia (Bintliff, 1996a), we have achieved this goal with a small, largely enclosed upland valley landscape, where in the long-term there has normally only been one nucleated settlement. Complete intensive survey of the Valley found some 50 archaeological sites of all periods from Neolithic to late Turkish times. In Greco-Roman antiquity the central nucleation was a large village or small town at Askra, which was particularly flourishing and extensive in Late Roman times (4th-6th centuries a.D.). Securely-dated Byzantine ceramics from Askra are of types current from the 9th-11th centuries a.D., but suggest a much smaller village in spatial terms, and are associated with a very large church in the centre of the site (Bintliff and Snodgrass, 1988). Our Project Byzantine historian–Archie Dunn, has argued that this community and its church can be identified with a settlement which gained an Orthodox bishop in the 12th century, who was then replaced after the early 13th century Frankish conquest of Greece with a Latin bishop. Direct archaeological evidence for continuity of use of the site between the 7th and 10th centuries is problematic, since characteristic medieval glazed and painted wares seem to be a novelty in the Greek provinces belonging to the 9th-11th centuries and not earlier. Our current thinking echoes that amongst many researchers working on the Mediterranean Late Antique to Medieval transition in both Byzantine and Islamic regions, that the transitional period may be characterised by considerable continuity of preceding material culture (notably ceramics). Our Byzantine ceramic specialist in Boeotia, Joanita Vroom, has thus modified her phase distributions of sites so that we now have a single 'Late Roman-Early Byzantine' era into which sites suggested to be either or both are classified, so as to introduce the strong possibility that 'Late Roman' ceramic styles were the main forms in use in the period after the 7th century a.D., and possibly up till the introduction of the distinctive novelties of the 9th-11th century ceramic repertoire (Early Byzantine is here dated between the mid-7th and mid-9th centuries a.D.).

Although this argument can offer a reason to postulate that the small Middle Byzantine (mid-9th to early 13th century) village of Askra –which significantly overlies the core of the Late Roman large community– may well have been its direct descendant, the archival sources both offer deeper confirmation but also a potential disconfirmation at one and the same time. The creation of a Suffragan bishop in the 12th century is at a place now called Zaratoba rather than Askra, and this has to indicate a dominant linguistic presence of Slav-speakers there. This should not surprise, since the majority of the Greek landscape was conquered by migrating Slav tribes in the late 6th and 7th centuries, leaving only major towns and fortresses in the hands of the Byzantine Empire (Malingoudis, 1991). Boeotia was recovered by the Byzantine army during the 8th-9th centuries. The toponym therefore ought to belong to the settlement of Slavs exactly at the period where our ceramic evidence is still ambiguous for continuity of site use at Askra. At the same time as giving us further cause for arguing for the site being continuously occupied, the replacement of a Greco-Roman with a Slav ethnic toponym might mean rather abandonment and a refoundation by new settlers on precisely the same spot within a reasonably short time. It is however far more likely that the Greco-Roman rural population of the Balkans was neither exterminated nor fled to the shrinking major cities and forts which escaped Slav control, but merged –perhaps peacefully– with the invaders, creating Slavo-Hellenic countrysides. Askra should in any case have shrunk with the warfare and plagues of the 6th-7th centuries but subsequently have received additional population from the Slav settlement. It recovered sufficiently to be awarded its own bishop in the 12th century. Growth continued into the 12th and 13th centuries, or High Middle Ages, as can be seen in the quantities of both ceramic discard at sites such as this with earlier beginnings and also through the foundation of increasing numbers of sites with this date throughout those parts of Boeotia where we have carried out intensive survey (Bintliff, 1996).

The High Middle Ages and the Impact of the Frankish Conquest

As was noted earlier, the regional monuments in Boeotia suggest considerable continuity of the Greco-Roman settlement network into the High Middle Ages. Ancient towns and villages often seem to survive as hamlets or villages, whether or not their inhabitants remained in place, or were replaced, or supplemented, by Slav incomers. Thus when the Fourth Crusade conquers the Byzantine Imperial capital of Constantinople, and Mainland Greece is carved into a nested series of feudal fiefs under a Frankish elite, we are not now surprised to find that the dominant castles and the subfief markers of rural towers typically lie on or near ancient population centres (Bintliff, 1995, 1997). The regional castles at Thebes and Livadhia were ancient cities, the former probably remaining in Byzantine hands through the Dark Ages. The feudal towers seem to have been placed as defended points of surplus extraction from nearby indigenous villages, and show little attempt to occupy remote defensive positions or those with good intervisibility between each other.

A good example can be given through continuing the historical story for the Valley of the Muses (Bintliff, 1996a). Probably early in the 13th century, a feudal tower is erected about 500 m distant from the Byzantine village of Askra, and at this time the majority of the villagers seem to have been moved to a hillside immediately below that tower. Arguably the Latin bishop remained at Askra, and may have been the object of regular predation by the minor feudal occupier of the tower, to judge by correspondence which our Project Frankish historian

Peter Lock believes is associated with these localities (Lock, 1995). The new village site (site VM4 in our survey numbering) shows a more extensive area than Byzantine Askra, reflecting that longer-term growth of population in the countryside we saw commencing in the 10th-11th centuries a.D. (Bintliff, 1997).

Catastrophe and Recovery-The Fourteenth to Sixteenth Centuries

The central village in the Valley of the Muses, formerly at Askra-Zaratoba at the ancient and Byzantine location, now at the new location of VM4 –of uncertain naming in the Frankish era, gives from archaeological intensive survey a clear picture of dramatically-enhanced population growth from the 14th-16th centuries (the Late Frankish and Early Ottoman era). At the end of that period this village –which by now is certainly called Panagia– is greater in extent than ancient Askra at its maximum (12 compared to 10.5 ha) and is known to house over 1000 people. The ceramic evidence from VM4 (Bintliff, 1997; Vroom, 1999), is in the form of a maximum extent of wares of Late Frankish-Early Turkish styles, dated to these three centuries. Moreover the prosperity of Panagia can be further evidenced not only by its foreign import wares (from Italy and Anatolia), but also from the Ottoman tax archive records (defters), translated by our Project Ottomanist Prof. Machiel Kiel (Bintliff, 1995; Kiel, 1997), where alongside those population figures we see that the village was wealthy enough to fund two new monasteries and some half-dozen water-mills in its territory.

The potential of the Ottoman archives is extraordinary for rural history and archaeology in all of its former provinces. Professor Kiel and I have been able to locate some 75% of the archive villages for Boeotia, and this does offer a very rich means of comparing surface material traces with highly-detailed inventories for each community at a number of time-intervals from 1466 to 1687. It is clear that the early Ottoman era of the late 15th and 16th centuries was a time of stability and rapid growth of population and economic production in our region –due in large part to the benefits of the Pax Ottomanica.

However, it is exactly these records but on the level of the entire province, which give us a more subtely-complex story to that detectable from VM4-Panagia for the transition from Frankish to Ottoman times. The 1466 Ottoman tax register is the first so far available, and it provides clear evidence for the aftermath of a catastrophic depopulation. If we begin with villages classed as equivalent to Byzantine Orthodox Greek, only a small number are present, mostly clustered in the fringes of the central mountains of the province (one being Panagia-VM4). These are large. Elsewhere there is a wide dispersal of small recent settlements described as Arnavaudan –or Albanian, and furthermore termed "katuns" which signifies semi-mobile communities. Textual sources inform us (Jochalas, 1971), that in the final Frankish period and the Early Ottoman era a major wave of Albanian colonists was invited to settle in South-Central Greece to repopulate the land. The reasons for such largescale loss of villages must include the known impact of the mid-14th century Black Death, constant warfare in this region, and raids by Ottoman pirates from the coastlands. If we take away these new colonists we see that over two-thirds of the Byzantine-Frankish settlements must have been abandoned, probably largely in the 14th century. The large size of the few survivor indigenous villages, such as Panagia, must reflect their status as refuge communities for wider areas.

The subsequent tax records show that the Albanian hamlets multiplied and grew larger, and the Greek villages also grew even further. The katuns became permanent villages with tree crops and other products comparable to the Greek settlements. Given the disturbed conditions of the final Frankish centuries, this picture of growth and prosperity is attributable to the improved conditions consequent upon the imposition of the "Pax Ottomanica" (Kiel, 1997).

The Decline of the Ottoman Empire and the Origins of the Traditional Villages of Today, Seventeenth to Nineteenth Centuries

The tax records agree very well with the field survey evidence in evidencing a dramatic decline of the region during the 17th century a.D. (Bintliff, 1995; Kiel, 1997). Villages are abandoned or contract considerably in size, and most are converted from semi-autonomous communities paying taxes to support the Ottoman military elite, into serf-estates or *ciftliks*. The village of Panagia-VM4 for example (Bintliff, 1996a, 1997; Vroom, 1999) has very little surface ceramic evidence for the later Turkish era (17th century and later), but we know from the tax records that it shrank dramatically in size (to some one third of its 16th century population) and was broken up into twelve small serf-estates. In fact other sources tell us that the main village location was abandoned for a new one some 2 km distant, where the modern village still lies.

These troubles were in fact general throughout the Ottoman Empire (Inalcik, 1972), and were the complex result of a number of historical factors –the decline of imperial administration, radical transformations to the army and hence the peasant tax system in response to the challenge of Western military technology, the progressive undermining of the Ottoman economy by Western capitalism, the effects of a series of crippling wars, and climatic deterioration.

A fortunate discovery promises to shed light on the new situation in the countryside from an archaeological viewpoint. For many years our Project team in Boeotia resided in the village of Mavrommati. Part of that village's population was traditionally believed to have migrated there from a now deserted village called Harmena. We were shown the spot and it also subsequently appeared in the Ottoman village tax records. Most remarkable was the chance discovery by Machiel Kiel of a rare late tax record for this community –an 18th century assessment (Kiel, 1997). Here it is described as a great ciftlik, and indeed its population is considerable for its era –some 200-300 inhabitants. We are interested to see exactly what material conditions were like in such a serf-estate, a form of tied cultivation which at least by the early 19th century was giving rise to very negative comments by Western travellers within the Ottoman Empire. The ceramic finds from the surface of Harmena are surprisingly rich and varied, rather than cheap homemade coarseware which one might have expected from such a community. However, the standing buildings at the village (abandonment must have occurred before the 19th century) do match early modern descriptions and drawings for ciftliks (eg Cvijic, 1918): we have made architectura plans of a large number of rather primitive rubble foundation longhouses and one much more pretentious, multiple-storey house, which must represent peasant families and the estate owner or supervisor respectively. On the positive side though, is the mention in the 18th tax record of a group of people living in the ciftlik who were there voluntarily as additional workers.

The early 19th century saw massive disruption to rural life with the War of Independence, but even after the foundation of the modern Greek state at the end of the 1820s a further half-century of economic depression ensued –with severe problems over land distribution and endemic banditry in Boeotia (Slaughter and Kasimis, 1986). During this time it seems that many villages which had survived into the 17th-18th centuries, or were founded as part of the transformation into ciftiks, were abandoned and their inhabitants moved into a smaller number of villages. We are currently studying the surface finds from several such recent deserted villages (Bintliff, 1995, 1997; Vroom, 1996, 1997, 1998). Finally the last quarter of the 19th century witnessed a phenomenal population boom focussed on these larger villages, one paralleled in almost all the rural zones of the Mediterranean lands. More secure conditions and the impact of commercial agriculture, a rise in rural industrial production (Proto-Industrialisation), and the improvements in maritime and overland communications, are amongst the critical factors. One material symptom is the arrival in quantity during this period either side of 1900 of relatively inexpensive factory-produced ceramics into rural villages, including foreign imports from Western Europe (Vroom, 1998).

BEYOND CHRONOLOGY AND HISTOIRE ÉVÉNEMENTIELLE

Although as has been seen, there remain problems of ceramic chronology and ethnic history for future research, the evidence of surface survey, combined with the rich archive materials, does allow us to address other historical issues beyond the essential reconstruction of the historical geography of the region. These deal with the additional information we can hope to extract from material culture of the medieval and postmedieval eras.

First.–*housing*. We have observed that the basic peasant house at 18th century Harmena was a single-storey longhouse. Current work at the Frankish-Early Ottoman deserted village of Panagia-VM4, where there are fragments of house outlines, may show whether this standard house type for Boeotian villages in the Early Modern era already existed by the 16th century. It is specific to a form of open plan settlement with stock in part sharing the longhouse with the family, whilst both traces of this plan and of the house type survive in most older villages of South-Central Greece (but sadly will not for long) (Dimitsantou-Kremezi, 1996). Descriptions and occasional depictions of house interiors of this kind of dwelling in normal use during the 19th century show it to be relatively unfurnished and lacking in signs of wealth both in construction and house contents. Apart from documenting the houses visible at deserted villages, we have also studied standing examples in traditional villages (eg. Stedman, 1996), as well as carrying out a programme of recording pre-modern vernacular constructions in the provincial capital of Livadhia (where the longhouse was also surprisingly common alongside the multistorey larger dwellings of the middle and upper classes) (Aalen et al., 1999). Apart from the ubiquitous traces of watermills and irrigation conduits of the Ottoman era, and the churches, castles and towers discussed earlier, other Medieval-Postmedieval architectural remains are rare in Mainland Greece. The example of a small mosque in the former main street of Livadhia, its shell occuped by a flower-shop, is typical of the arbitrary nature of survival of once major monuments.

Next.–*the ceramic assemblage as social history.* We are currently, particularly through the researches of our Project post-Classical pottery specialist Joanita Vroom *(op. cit.)*, investigating the potential of the rich and well-preserved ceramic collections from the survey's surface sites, to shed light on changing wealth, trade and lifestyles amongst the rural communities of Central Greece. A particular inspiration was a pioneering paper on Italian medieval survey ceramics by Hugo Blake (1980), which dealt with the evidence they offered for the relative wealth of different settlements. An additional aspect of social history relates to the story of dining habits in Europe. Our medieval assemblages are comparable to those of other South European countries such as Italy and Spain, where older traditions of communal eating from wide open shared serving dishes were being supplemented from the late 15th century by individual bowls and plates for each diner. Whilst however this tendency in Western Europe was to develop further in association with the rise of Capitalism and Individualism, resulting in a full suite of personal ceramics, glasses and table cutlery (cf. Gaimster, 1994), Greece shifted during Ottoman times into Oriental eating (both in culinary terms and in table manners): once again large open shapes in the centre of tables served a group of diners, who had limited personal tableware and cutlery. Careful analysis of our large ceramic assemblages is currently being carried out to trace the timing and extent of these changes in eating habits, with the aid of contemporary scenes in art (notably church icons, which frequently modify biblical depictions to suit changing table customs!).

By the time that Western factory-produced tableware began to pour into the Greek countryside, in the final decades of the 19th century, the orientation of rural life was once again facing westwards –so that rapidly we see the adoption of modern styles of individual eating as required by the ceramic sets being supplied. A parallel process was taking place at the Sultan's table in Istanbul from the 19th century, with vast dinner services being made to order from the West.

BIBLIOGRAPHY

AALEN, F., BINTLIFF, J., SIGALOS E., SPOERRY, P. (1999): *H paradosiaki, topiki architektoniki tis Livadeias,* in Dimos Levadeon (ed.), Symposio, H Livadeia Chthes, Simera, Avrio, Livadeia, pp. 85-103.

BINTLIFF, J.L. (1994): "The history of the Greek countryside: As the wave breaks, prospects for future research", in P.N. Doukellis and L.G. Mendoni (eds.), *Structures Rurales et Societes Antiques,* Paris, Les Belles Lettres, pp. 7-15.

BINTLIFF, J.L. (1995): "The Two Transitions: Current Research on the Origins of the Traditional Village in Central Greece", in J.L. Bintliff and H. Hamerow (eds.), *Europe Between Late Antiquity and the Middle Ages. Recent Archaeological and Historical Research in Western and Southern Europe,* Oxford, Tempus Reparatum, BAR International Series 617, pp. 111-130.

BINTLIFF, J.L. (1996a): "The archaeological survey of the Valley of the Muses and its significance for Boeotian History", in A. Hurst and A. Schachter (eds.), *La Montagne des Muses,* Geneva, Librairie Droz, pp. 193-224.

BINTLIFF, J.L. (1996b): "The Frankish countryside in central Greece: The evidence from archaeological field survey", in P. Lock and G.D.R. Sanders (eds.), *The Archaeoloy of Medieval Greece,* Oxford, Oxbow, pp. 1-18.

BINTLIFF, J.L. (1997): "The archaeological investigation of deserted medieval villages in Greece", in G.D. Boe and F. Verhaege (eds.), *Rural Settlements in Medieval Europe. Papers of the "Medieval Europe Brugge 1997",* Conference, Vol. 6, Zellik, Archaeological Institute for the Heritage, pp. 21-34.

BINTLIFF, J.L., SNODGRASS, A.M. (1988): "Mediterranean survey and the city", *Antiquity,* 62, pp. 57-71.

BLAKE, H. (1980): "Technology, supply or demand?", *Medieval Ceramics,* 4, pp. 3-12.

BOMMELJÉ, Y., DOORN, P. (1996): "The long and winding road: land routes in Aetolia (Greece) since Byzantine times", in H. Kamermans and K. Fennema (eds.), *Interfacing the Past. Analecta Praehistorica Leidensia,* 28, Leiden, pp. 343-351.

CVIJIC, J. (1918): *La Peninsule Balkanique,* Paris, Armand Colin.

DIMITSANTOU-KREMEZI, A. (1996): *Attiki. Elliniki Paradosiaki Architektoniki,* Melisa Press, Athens.

ELLENBLUM, R. (1998): *Frankish rural settlement in the Latin Kingdom of Jerusalem,* CUP.

ELLENBLUM, R., RUBIN, R., SOLAR, G. (1996): "Khirbat al-Lawza, a Frankish farm house in the Judaean Hills in Central Palestine", *Levant,* 28, pp. 189-198.

FRANTZ, M.A. (1942): "Turkish pottery from the Agora", *Hesperia,* 1942, 11, pp. 1-28.

GAIMSTER, D. (1994): "The archaeology of Post-Medieval society, c.1450-1750: Material culture studies in Britain since the War", in B. Vyner (ed.), *Building on the Past. Papers Celebrating 150 Years of the Royal Archaeological Institute,* The Royal Archaological Institute, London, pp. 283-312.

HAYES, J.W. (1992): *Excavations at Saraçhane in Istanbul. II: The Pottery,* Princeton and Washington.

INALCIK, H. (1972): "The Ottoman decline and its effect upon the Reaya", in H. Birnbaum and S. Vryonis (eds.), *Aspects of the Balkans, Continuity and Change,* Mouton, the Hague, pp. 338-354.

JOCHALAS, T. (1971): "Über die Einwanderung der Albaner in Griechenland", *Beiträge zur Kenntnis Sudosteuropas und des nahen Orients,* 13, pp. 89-106.

KIEL, M. (1997): "The rise and decline of Turkish Boeotia, 15th-19th century. Remarks on the settlement pattern, demography and agricultural production according to unpublished Ottoman-Turkish census- and taxation records", in J.L. Bintliff (ed.), *Recent Developments in the History and Archaeology of Central Greece,* British Archaeological Reports, Int. Ser. 666, Oxford, pp. 315-358.

KIEL, M. (1999): "The icon and the mosque: Orthodox Christian art as a source to retrieve the lost monuments of Ottoman architecture of Southern Greece. The case of Istife / Thebes", in C. Kafesoglu and L. Thys-Senocak (eds.), *Aptullah Kuran icin Yazilar / Essays in Honour of Aptullah Kuran,* Yapi Kredi Yayinlari, Istanbul, pp. 223-232.

KODER, J., HILD, F. (1976): *Hellas und Thessalia,* Wien, Österreichische Akademie der Wissenschaften.

KUNA, M. (1991): "The structuring of prehistoric landscape", *Antiquity,* 65, pp. 332-347.

LEHMANN, H. (1939): "Die Siedlungsräume Ostkretas", *Geographische Zeitschrift,* 45, pp. 212-228.

LOCK, P. (1986): "The Frankish towers of Central Greece", *Annual of the British School at Athens,* 81, pp. 101-123.

LOCK, P. (1995): *The Franks in the Aegean 1204-1500,* London, Longman.

LOCK, P. (1996): "The towers of Euboea: Lombard or Venetian, agrarian or strategic", in P. Lock and G.D.R. Sanders (eds.), *The Archaeology of Medieval Greece,* Oxbow Books, Oxford, pp. 106-126.

MALINGOUDIS, Ph. (1991): *Slavi sti Mesaioniki Ellada,* Ekdoseis Banias, Thessaloniki.

MORGAN, C.H. (1942): *Corinth, XI: The Byzantine Pottery,* Cambridge Massachusetts, 1942.

PAPANIKOLA-BAKIRTZI, D. (1999): *Byzantine Ephialomena Keramika. Edosi tou Tameiou Archaeiologikon Poron ke Apallotrioseon,* Athens.

SANDERS, G.D.R. (1987): "An assemblage of Frankish pottery from Corinth", *Hesperia,* 56, 159-195.

SANDERS, G.D.R. (1995): *Byzantine Glazed Pottery at Corinth to c. 1125,* PhD dissertation, University of Birmingham, U.K.

SANDERS, G.D.R. (1996): "Two kastra on Melos and their relations in the Archipelago", in P. Lock and G.D.R. Sanders (eds.), *The Archaeology of Medieval Greece,* Oxbow Books, Oxford, pp. 148-177.

SLAUGHTER, C., KASIMIS, C. (1986): "Some social-anthropological aspects of Boeotian rural society: A field report", *Byzantine and Modern Greek Studies,* 10, pp. 103-159.

STEDMAN, N. (1996): "Land-use and settlement in post-medieval central Greece: An interim discussion", in P. Lock and G.D.R. Sanders (eds.), *The Archaeology of Medieval Greece,* Oxbow Books, Oxford, 179-192.

VROOM, J. (1996): "Coffee and archaeology. A note on a Kutahya Ware find in Boeotia, Greece. Pharos", *Journal of the Netherlands Institute at Athens,* IV, pp. 5-19.

VROOM, J. (1997): "Pots and pans: New perspectives on medieval ceramics in Greece", in G. De Boe and F. Verhaeghe (ed.), *Material Culture in Medieval Europe. Papers of the "Medieval Europe Brugge 1997",* Conference, Vol. 7, Bruges, Zellik, pp. 203-213.

VROOM, J. (1998): "Early Modern archaeology in Central Greece: The contrast of Artefact-Rich and Sherdless Sites", *Journal of Mediterranean Archaeology,* 11, 2, pp. 131-164.

VROOM, J. (1999): "Medieval and Post-Medieval Pottery From a Site in Boeotia: A Case Study Example of Post-Classical Archaeology in Greece", *Annual of the British School at Athens,* 92, pp. 513-546.

WHITELAW, T.M. (1991): "The ethnoarchaeology of recent rural settlement and land use in Northwest Keos", in J.F. Cherry, J.C. Davis and E. Mantzourani (eds.), *Landscape Archaeology as Long-Term History,* Los Angeles, Institute of Archaeology, University of California, pp. 403-454.

LES NOUVELLES QUESTIONS DE LA PROBLÉMATIQUE DES CHÂTEAUX DE L'EUROPE CENTRALE

LESZEK KAJZER
Institut d'Archéologie, Université de Tódà (Pologne)

La partie centrale de l'Europe évoquée dans le titre est une région non pas définie jusqu'au bout. Dans diverses périodes elle a été considérée d'une façon différente, ce qui a été influencé par d'autres conditionnements politiques et géographiques. Après la I guerre mondiale la dénomination "Mitteleuropa" comprenait tout simplement toutes les terres qui étaient jusqu'alors sous la domination de la familler des Habsburg. Après la II guerre mondiale l'Europe a été divisée en partie "est", arrivant jusqu'au fleuve d'Elbe étant sous la domination de l'URSS et partie "occidentale" comprenant les pays démocratiques. Cette division a été conditionnée quand même politiquement, et non géographiquement et historiquement. Actuellement, après la normalisation de la situation sur notre continent il est plus facile de définir les divisions traditionnelles. Le plus souvent on considère comme l'Europe centrale le territoire à l'est du Rhin et à l'ouest de la Vistule/Boug et à nord du cours du Danube. Le territoire limité par ces grands fleuves comprend de grandes parties de "l'Europe germanique" et presque toute la ainsi-dite Europe mineure, c'est-à-dire les pays avec la prédomination de l'élément slave (J. Kłoczowski, 1998) jusqu'à la base de la Péninsule des Balkans. Pour les buts de l'analyse de la problématique des châteaux médiévaux ce territoire est décisément trop étendu. Les sièges de défense y créés dans le bas Moyen-âge étaient très différenciés en tant que provenant de différentes traditions européennes (et locales) de construction et d'architecture. C'est pourquoi dans la présente analyse je vais m'occuper d'un territoire beaucoup moins étendu, correspondant environ à l'espace actuel de l'Allemagne, de la Bohème, de la Slovaquie et de la Pologne.

II

Déjà au XIX siècle la science française et allemande ont élaboré des méthodes d'analyse historique et architecturale des châteaux médiévaux. Ce qui est particulièrement important pour les buts de ce texte ce sont les longues et brillantes traditions des investigateurs allemands des châteaux du XIX, et en particulier du XX siècle (O. Piper, 1912; B. Ebhardt, 1939; A. Tuulse, 1958; C. Tillmann, 1960;

W. Hotz, 1965). Parmi les travaux plus récents il faut mentionner les études de T. Biller sur les châteaux privés (T. Biller, 1993) et de W.H. Böhme (1991) sur les places de défense de l'époque des empereurs de la dynastie salicienne. Une attention particulière est due aux deux livres plus récents, qui méritent une discussion plus détaillée. Le premier d'eux, écrit par F.W. Krahe (1996), est le lexique des châteaux allemands contenant les informations sur 4056 châteaux. Bien que ce livre ait eu déjà un large compterendu (J. Salm, 1996, pp. 331-335), il exige d'être mentionné ici aussi. L'auteur a adopté les limites du territoire décrit d'après la littérature plus ancienne, principalement d'après C. Tillmann. Il décrit donc les châteaux qui se trouvent dans les limites administratifs des actuels territoires de l'Allemagne, de l'Autriche et des cantons de langue allemande de la Suisse, des anciennes propriétés autrichiennes en Slovenie, Lichtenstein, Luxembourg, Alsacie et Lotaryngie, Bohème et Moravie. En ce qui concerne le territoire polonais, l'auteur a pris en considération les châteaux de la Silésie et de la Poméranie, et dans le bordereau à part –les châteaux des ordres chevaleresques de la Pologne nord-orientale, de l'arrondissement de Kaliningrad (Russie), de la Lettonie et de l'Estonie. Selon ses estimations sur ce territoire, de la surface de 600.000 km^2 environ on a bâti 17.500 châteaux, dont 13.000 fonctionnaient simultanément. Dans l'analyse typologique menée du point de vue de la topographie des châteaux l'auteur a distingué 3 groupes fondamentaux: les châteaux de plaine, les châteaux de haut-plateau et les châteaux de roche. En outre l'auteur a fait l'analyse des différentes parties constituant des châteaux (les murs entourant, les différents types de tours, les bâtiments principaux, les bâtiments accessoires, les chapelles, les puits, les avant-châteaux, etc.). La partie principale du travail (pp. 51-690) est constituée naturellement par le catalogue, où en outre de courtes descriptions on trouve les plans des murs des châteaux avec l'indication du relief du sol. Les plans des châteaux ne contiennent pas malheureusement les couches chronologiques des murs bâtis successivement. La valeur principale du travail de F.W. Krahe, malgré ses défauts évidents (v. J. Salm, 1996) consiste en rassemblement d'une grande quantité du matériel comparatif, qui exige peut-être d'être vérifié, mais d'autre part permet de conduire des recherches plus détaillées et plus profondes.

Le travail suivant, c'est l'étude sous la rédaction de H.W. Böhme, l'auteur du travail sur les places de défense de l'époque des empereurs de la dynastie salicienne (H.W. Böhme, et autres, réd. 1998) mentionné ci-dessus. À la différence du livre de F.W. Krahe elle n'a pas le caractere du catalogue de châteaux muni d'un large commentaire. C'est un rassemblement encyclopédique de l'état de recherche sur le château de l'Europe Centrale. L'auteur est le redacteur du libre (ainsi que les auteurs des entres concernant les régions différentes) sous la dénomination de "Mitteleuropa" comprennent non seulement le territoire de l'Allemagne mais aussi la Scandinavie méridionale, les Pays Bas, la Belgique, la Suisse, l'Autriche et la Bohème (avec la Moravie). Quant au territoire polonais le travail mentionné ci-dessus prend en considération seulement les provinces occidentales, c'est-à-dire la Silésie, la Poméranie occidentale et la région nord-orientale, correspondante au territoire de l'État des Chevaliers Teutoniques. La diversité de l'architecture des châteaux des Chevaliers Teutoniques est d'ailleurs remarquée par tous les chercheurs et dans le présent texte elle va être discutée à part. L'encyclopédie du savoir sur les châteaux médiévaux (parce que c'est ainsi qu'il faut considérer le livre publié sous la rédaction de H.W. Böhme) et le travail de F.W. Krahe mentionné ci-dessus malgré l'évidente diversité entre eux informent tous les deux de la grande importance de la littérature de la langue allemande dans la connaissance des châteaux sur le territoire de l'Europe centrale en question.

Sous l'influence des traditions de la science allemande se sont dévéloppées aussi les recherches sur les châteaux de la Bohème. Bien que la castellologie tchèque et ses conditionnements européens soient présentés il y a peu de temps par T. Durdik (T. Durdik, 1998a, pp. 784-789), le problème exige une courte explication. Abstraction faite de nombreux travaux du XIX et XX s., l'étude de D. Menclova (D. Menclova, 1972) a été la première élaboration synthétique, et –bien qu'elle soit publiée avec vingt ans de retard– elle constitue jusqu'aujourd'hui le précis fondamental des changements architecturaux et stylistiques des châteaux bohémiens. La méthodologie de recherches contemporaines sur les châteaux bohémiens a été élaborée au début des années'70. L'interdisciplinarité est constitue son caractére principal. Le château est perçu comme un complexe ayant une forme et une fonction, sujet à un développement dynamique. La problématique du niveau actuel de recherches et de besoins scientifiques a été ébauchée déjà en 1976 par T. Durdik (T. Durdik, 1976, pp. 172-180). Le même auteur a élaboré récemment une brève encyclopédie des châteaux bohémiens (T. Durdik, 1995). Les nouveaux travaux concernent aussi bien de grandes constructions, surtout des châteaux royaux du XIII siècle, que de petites forteresses ayant le caractère des maisons-fortes de chevaliers (Tvrze…, 1998). Leur développemnt allait des constructions en bois et en terre du type "motte" aux modernes résidences de la renaissance et du baroque. Quant à l'architecture de grands châteaux, les travaux sûrement les plus intéressants et dignes de diffusion sont les récentes recherches sur les châteaux du type castel dans l'Europe centrale (T. Durdik, 1998b). Comme on sait, dans les années du règne du roi français Philippe II Auguste (1180-1223) s'est formé le type du château défini comme "château du type castel français". Ce type de châteaux est l'objet de nombreux travaux anciens et récents, que nous n'allons pas citer ici en nous limitant à mentionner les derniers travaux de J. Mesqui (J. Mesqui, 1991-1993, 1997).

Les châteaux du type castel français ont formé dans une grande mesure l'image de l'architecture de châteaux non seulement en France, mais aussi par ex. en Angleterre. Un autre genre de châteaux réguliers typiques pour la Ière moitié du XIII siècle était constitué par les châteaux de l'empereur Frédéric II construit dans l'Italie méridionale. Les influences françaises ont déterminé aussi l'image des châteaux royaux bohémiens construits sur l'initiative du roi Przemysł Ottokar II (+ 1278). T. Durdik (1998b) est l'auteur de la thèse très intéressante d'après laquelle sous l'influence des traditions françaises et locales dans l'Europe centrale s'est formé le groupe des "châteaux du type castel d'Europe centrale". Ces châteaux, typiques pour la Bohémie, existent aussi en Autriche et en Hongrie, et peut-être en Pologne en Basse Silésie. En Bohémie les édifices les plus connus et relativement bien conservés de ce groupe sont: le château encore "français" de Tyřov, celui, également français, de Konopište et les typiques châteaux du type castel d'Europe centrale: Kadaň, Pisek, Domažlice, Chrudim, Horšovsky Tyn et Litomiěřice. En Autriche il faut compter au nombre de ces châteaux du type castel d'Europe centrale Wien –Hofburg et Wien– Neustadt, et en Hongrie-Köszeg. Je reviendrai au problème des châteaux du type castel d'Europe centrale en parlant des châteaux de l'État des Chevaliers Teutoniques en Prussie et de la Basse Silésie en Pologne.

La Slovaquie est un pays de nombreux magnifiques et pitoresques châteaux, dont les plus intéressants sont le château de Bratislava, Zvolen, Trenčin et le château de Spiš, la grande forteresse des rois hongrois et leurs starostes. Bien que beaucoup de ces châteaux sont l'objet des études monographiques (D. Menclová, 1935, 1954, 1956, 1957) et la beauté des châteaux de la Slovaquie est connue grâce à de nombreux albums et publications (H. Fialova, A. Fiala, 1966; Š. Pisoń, 1973 et 1977), jusqu'à présent on n'a pas publié le catalogue fondamental des châteaux de cette région. C'est pourquoi pour bien connaitre les châteaux de la Slovaquie les études sur les châteaux hongrois ont une si grande importance (citons les travaux de L. Gerö, 1955, 1969, éd. 1975), étant donné que jusqu'à la Ière guerre mondiale toute cette région faisait partie de l'Hongrie.

Les châteaux polonais intéressaient les chercheurs déjà au XIXème siècle, mais seulement en 1974 a été publiée l'étude de B. Guerquin (B. Guerquin, 1974) presentantant l'état de recherche des transformations de châteaux polonais dans les années 60 du XXème siècle. Ce livre contient en plus des informations fondamentales sur plus de 450 châteaux les plus importants sur le territoire actuel de la République Polonaise. Le travail de B. Guerquin, qui avait publié auparavant le catalogue des châteaux de la Silésie, basé d'ailleurs en grande partie sur les résultats de recherches allemandes antérieures (B. Guerquin, 1957), a une grande valeur jusqu'à présent. Ce travail, réédité en 1984 est la plus complète publication sur les châteaux polonais. Vu quand-même qu'elle a apparu il y a déjà 25 ans, certaines données y contenues doivent être actualisées. Actuellement est en préparation le Lexicon des châteaux polonais (Lexicon...) rassemblant les informations fondamentales sur 500 châteaux polonais plus importants et un riche matériel illustratif.

Parmi d'autres travaux plus récents il faut mentionner la nouvelle publication sur les châteaux du sud de la Basse Silésie (A. Boguszewicz, en préparation). L'approche interdisciplinaire de cet auteur lui a permis de faire de nombreuses découvertes très intéressantes. Pour la première fois dans la littérature on a posé le problème des ainsi- dits châteaux romans, c'est-à-dire les premiers châteaux construits en pierres (et en briques) à la fin du XIIème et au XIIIème siècle. Jusqu'à présent on pensait, que le plus ancien château polonais était la forteresse du prince de la Silésie Henryk Brodaty (+ 1236) à Legnica. Le mérite de A. Boguszewicz est aussi l'identification des châteaux du type "de transition" du XIIIème siècle. C'etaient des constructions aussi bien en pierre qu'en bois bâties par les princes pour contrôler les colons des autres nations venus habiter en Silésie par la volonté des souverains. Les châteaux du type "des transitions" constituent un élélement important informant de la transformation du modèle de château en bois en château en pierre. La troisième remarque qu'il faut faire est la constatation que sous l'influence des châteaux du type d'Europe centrale un groupe spécifique des châteaux du type castel a été construit aussi sous le mécènat de princes de Świdnica.

Le problème des châteaux des Chevaliers Teutoniques en Prussie qui interéssait les chercheurs allemands pendant tout le XIXe siècle a provoqué que la littérature sur ce sujet est très large. Les travaux particulièrement importants sont ceux de: C. Steinbrecht (C. Steinbrecht, 1888-1920), K.H. Clasen (K.H. Clasen, 1927) et B. Schmid (B. Schmid, 1938). Après la deuxième guerre mondiale la majorité des châteaux des Chevaliers Teutoniques s'est trouvée dans les confins de la Pologne. Parmi les travaux polonais sur ce sujet (v. L. Kajzer, J. Salm, 1996) il faut mentionner avant tout les études de deux chercheurs de Toruń: J.Frycz et M.Arszyński (J. Frycz, 1978; M. Arszyński, 1970, 1995). Grâce à la normalisation de la coopération entre les historiens allemands et polonais T. Torbus (Torbus, 1998) a publié dernièrement en Allemagne un vaste libre dédié à la problématique des châteaux-couvents des Chevaliers Teutoniques, c'est-à-dire aux constructions des châteaux les plus magnifiques bâties par les Chevaliers Teutoniques des la moitié du XIIIe siècle au tournant des siècles XIV et XVe.

Le livre de T. Torbus qui rassemble le matériel historique et iconographique complet constitue une oeuvre dont l'importance est comparable à celle des travaux de C. Steinbrecht mentionnés ci-dessus.

Comme il n'y a pas de doutes que les châteaux-couvents des Chevaliers Teutoniques sont un des groupes des châteaux européens les plus magnifiques (comme par exemple les forteresses de Croisés dans la Terre Sainte) il vaut la peine de signaler ici la nouvelle classification des châteuax-couvents élaborée par T. Torbus. Il les a divisés en sept groupes: les châteaux les plus anciens (encore irréguliers) bâtis sur des forteresses (en bois et en terre) plus anciennnes. Le deuxième groupe est constitué par les premiers châteaux réguliers des plans allongés avec la tendance à trois ailes. Le troisième groupe comprend les premiers châteaux du type castel dans la région de Chełmno et le quatrième –les châteaux du type castel classiques. Le cinquième groupe est constitué par les châteaux hétérogènes du territoire de la Poméranie Orientale. Le sixième groupe contient les maisons des couvents tardifs construits au XIVs. sur des territoires du Sud-Est nouvellement organisés.

Finalement le dernier groupe à part est constitué par le château à Ragnet (Ragnit-actuellement Nieman) construit au tournant du XIV et XVs. Le livre de T. Torbus ne contient pas de nouvelles hypothèses sur la genèse de châteaux-couvents des Chevaliers Teutoniques, mais il rappelle la littérature plus ancienne et l'auteur de ce texte trouve particulièrement interessante la thèse de T. Durdik (Durdik, 1992) qui a remarque les liens des châteaux du type castel de l'Europe Centrale (construits sous le mécenat du Roi bohémien Przemysł Ottokar II) et a signalé la possibilité de leur influence sur la formation du type de châteaux-couvents des Chevaliers Teutoniques. Naturellement la thèse de T. Durdik même si elle est très probable, ne ferme pas la discussion permanente, qui dure depuis des années autour des modèles génetiques des châteaux teutoniques, en particulier du château-couvent qui est le plus important parmi eux

III

Le nombre des revues et des publications périodiques spécialisées, ainsi que des Associations Scientifiques, se préoccoupant exclusivement de la problématique de l'étude des châteaux dans les pays de l'Europe Centrale qui nous intéresse ici est aussi une information sur l'état de recherche dans ce domaine. Dernièrement H.W. Bohme (H.W. Bohme et autres, 1998, vol. II, pp. 350-352) a cité les Associations allemandes les plus importantes.

Hélas, ni en Pologne ni en Slovaquie, il n'y a pas de tels périodiques spécialisés. Par contre en Bohème il y a peu de temps on or publié le sixième volume du periodique "Castellologia Bohemica" édité à Prague par T. Durdik. Trés nombreuses (et trés importantes) sont les Associations regroupant les chercheurs de châteaux du territoire de l'Allemagne et les périodiques publiés par elles.

En resumé, je crois que nous savons plus sur les châteaux allemands et bohémiens que sur les châteaux polonais et slovaques. L'état de recherche sur ces derniers exige d'accélérer les travaux des recherches, aussi bien territoriaux qu'analytiques et de préparer de nouvelles publications.

BIBLIOGRAPHIE

ARSZYŃSKI, M. (1970): *Technika i organizacja budownictwa ceglanego w Prusach w końcu XIV i w pierwszej połowie XV wieku*, Warszawa.

ARSZYŃSKI, M. (1995): *Budownictwo warowne zakonu krzyżackiego w Prusach (1230-1454)*, Toruń.

BILLER, T. (1993): *Die Adelsburg in Deutschland. Entstehung, Form und Bedeutung*, München.

BOGUSZEWICZ, A. (en preparation): *Fortyfikacje południowego pogranicza księstwa świdnicko - jaworskiego w XIII i na początku XIV wieku*, Wrocław.

BÖHME, W.H. (ed.) (1991): *Burgen der Salierzeit, Bd.I In den nördlichen Landschaften des Reiches, Bd. II In den sűdlichen Landschaften des Reiches*, Sigmaringen.

BÖHME, W.H. (ed.) (1998): *Burgen in Mitteleuropa. Ein Handbuch*, Bd.I-II, Stuttgart.

CLASEN, K.H. (1927): *Die mittelalterliche Kunst im Gebiete des Deutscheordensland, Bd.I, Burgbauten*, Königsberg

DURDIK, T. (1976): "Současny stav, potřeby a výhledy výzkumu hradu v Čechách", *Arch. Rozhledy*, XXVIII, Praha, pp. 172-180.

DURDIK, T. (1992): "French influence in Bohemian Castle architecture of the thirteenth Century", *Fortress*, 15, Hants, s. 16-30.

DURDIK, T. (1995): *Encyklopedie českých hradu*, Praha.

DURDIK, T. (1998a): "Česká kastellologie v evropských souvislostech", *Arch. Rozhledy*, Praha.

DURDIK, T. (1998b): *Hrady kastelového typu 13. stoleci ve středni Evropě*, Praha.

EBHARDT, B. (1939): *Der Wehrbau Europas im Mittelalters*, Oldenburg.

FIALOVA, H., FIALA, A. (1966): *Hrady na Slovensku*, Martin.

FRYCZ, J. (1978): "Architektura zamków krzyżackich", en: *Sztuka Pobrzeża Bałtyku*, Warszawa, pp. 20-48.

GERÖ, L., (1955): *Magyarországi várépiteszet*, Budapest.

GERÖ, L. (1969): *Castles in Hungary*, Budapest.

GERÖ, L. (ed.) (1975): *Várépiteszetűnk*, Budapet.

GUERQUIN, B. (1957): *Zamki śląskie*, Warszawa.

GUERQUIN, B. (1974): *Zamki w Polsce*, Warszawa, II éd. 1984.

HOTZ, W. (1965): *Kleine Kunstgeschichte der Deutschenland Burg*, Darmstadt.

KAJZER, L. (1993): *Zamki i społeczeństwo*, Łódź.

KAJZER, L., SALM, J. (1996): "Polnische Forschungen űber die Burgen im Gebiet des ehemaligen Deutschordensstadtes. Ein Bilanz derletzten 50 Jahre", *Castrum Bene*, Gdańsk, 5, pp. 73-95.

KŁOCZOWSKI, J. (1998): *Młodsza Europa. Europa środkowo-wschodnia w kręgu cywilizacji chrześciańskiej średniowiecza*, Warszawa.

KRAHE, F.W. (1996): *Burgen des deutschen Mittelalters. Grundriss-Lexicon*, Augsburg.

LEXICON... *Leksykon zamków w Polsce*, L. Kajzer, S. Kołodziejski, J. Salm, éd. L. Kajzer, Warszawa 2001.

MENCLOVÁ, D. (1935): *Hrad Bratislava*, Bratislava.

MENCLOVÁ, D. (1954): *Hrad Zvolen*, Bratislava.

MENCLOVÁ, D. (1956): *Hrad Trenčin*, Bratislava.

MENCLOVÁ, D. (1957): *Spišský hrad*, Bratislava.

MENCLOVÁ, D. (1972): *Česke hrady*, Praha.

MESQUI, J. (1991-1992): *Château et enceintes de la France médiévale. De la défense à la résidence. 1. Les organes de la défense, 2. La résidence et les éléments d'architecture*, Paris.

MESQUI, J. (1997): *Châteaux forts et fortifications en France*, Paris.

PIPER, O. (1912): *Burgenkunde*, Műnchen.

PISOŃ, S. (1973): *Hrady, zámky a kaštiele na Slovensku*, Martin, II ed. 1977.

SALM, J. (1996): "Le compte-rendu du livre de F.W. Krahe", en: *Kwartalnik Historii Kultury Materialnej*, XLIV, Warszawa, cahier 3, pp. 331-335.

TILLMANN, C. (1960): *Lexicon der Deutschen Burgen und Schlosser*, Bd.I-III, Stuttgart.

TORBUS, T. (1998): *Die Konventsburgen im Deutschordensland Preussen*, Műnchen.

TUULSE, A. (1958): *Burgen des Abendlandes*, Wien-München.

TVRZE... (1998): *Encyklopedie českých tvrzi, Bd.I, A-J*, L. Svoboda, J. Úlovec, P. Chotěbor et autres (éds.).

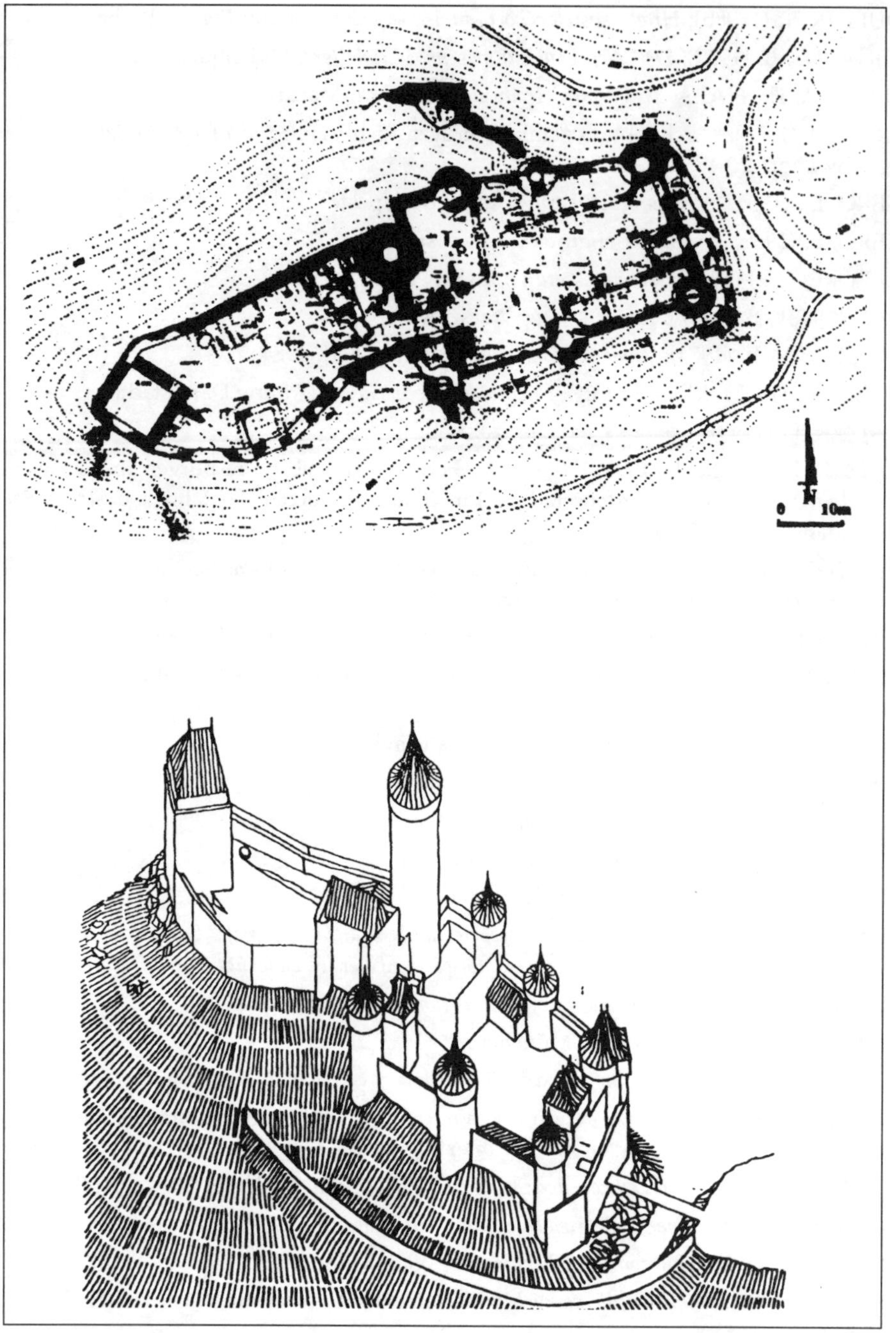

Fig. 1-1a. *Château du type castel français en Bohème. Le Château TYŘOV - le plan et la reconstruction de la masse, d'après T. Durdik, 1998B.*

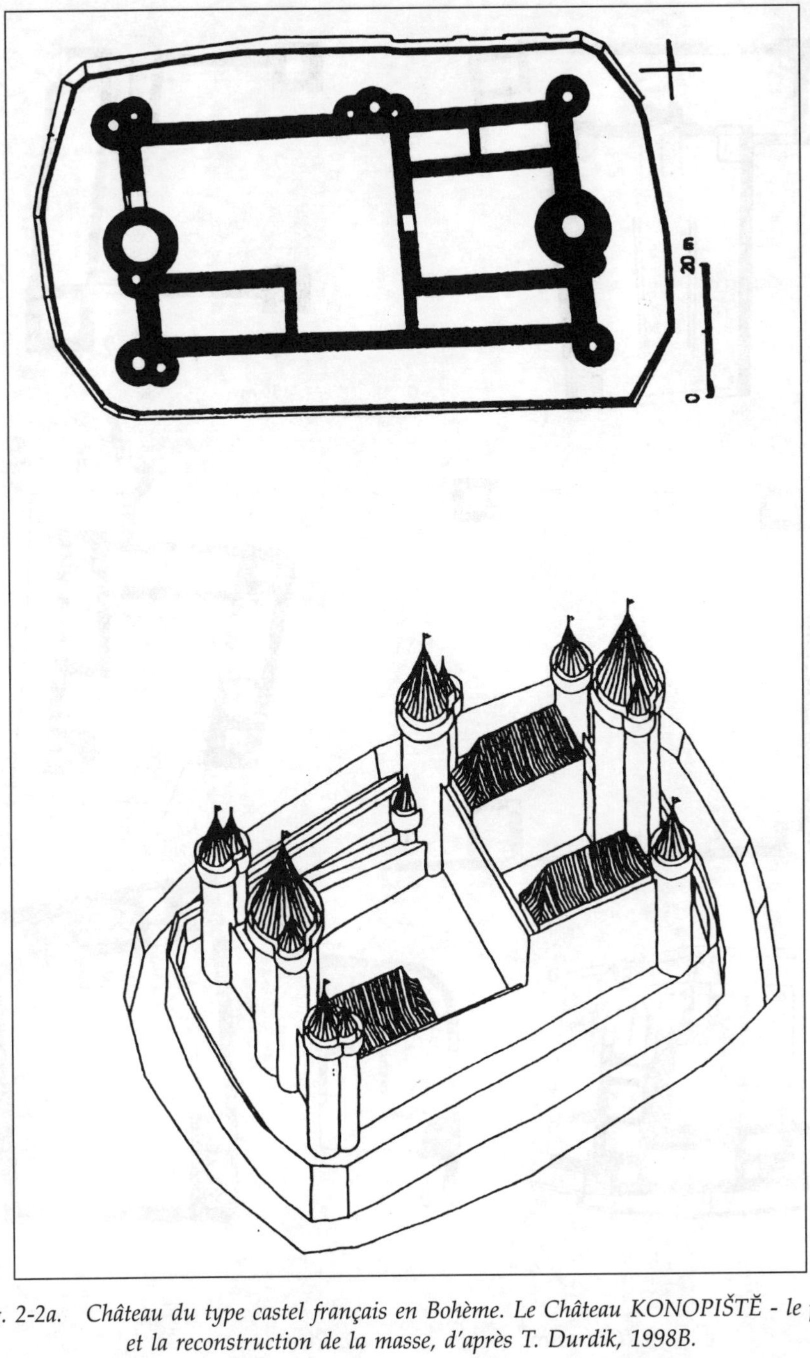

Fig. 2-2a. *Château du type castel français en Bohème. Le Château KONOPIŠTĚ - le plan et la reconstruction de la masse, d'après T. Durdik, 1998B.*

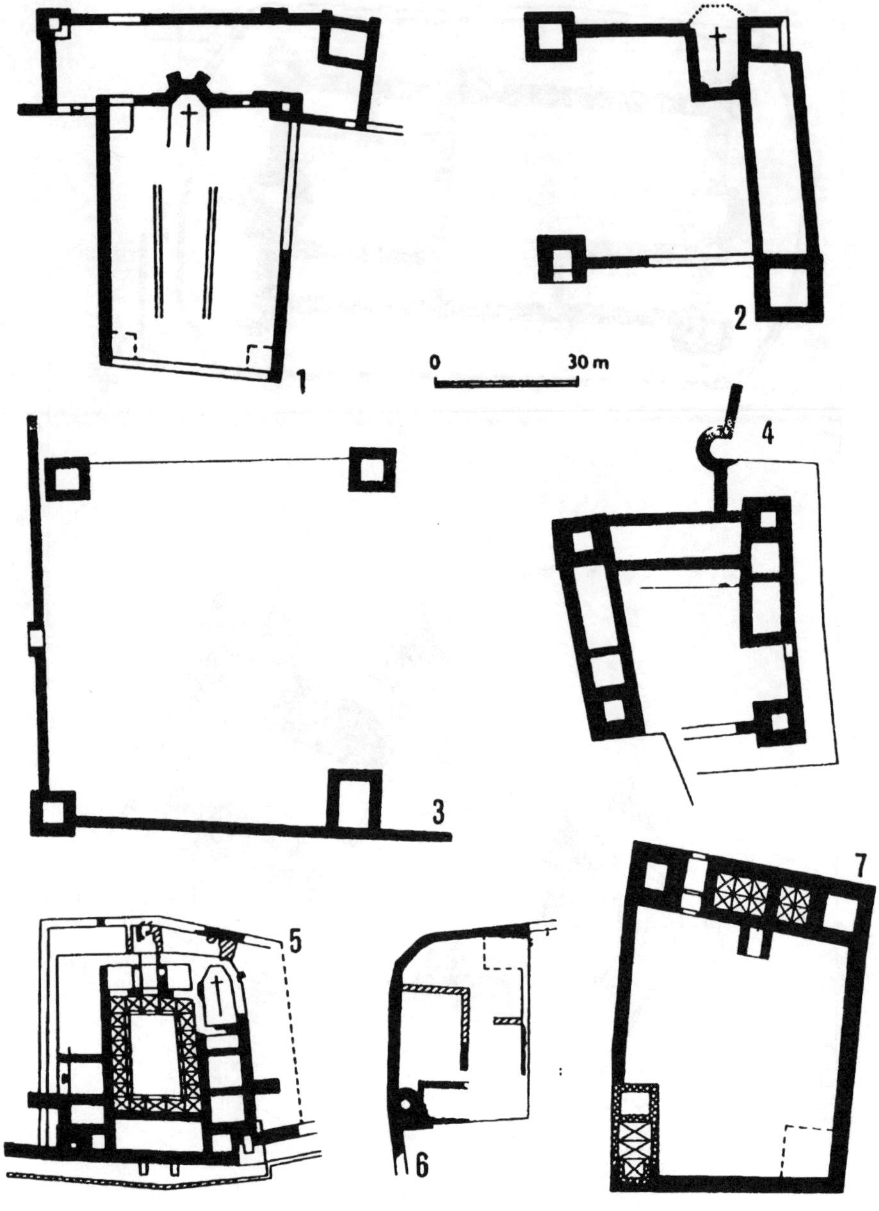

1. Chrudim
2. Wien
3. Wiener Neustadt
4. Kadaň
5. Pisek
6. Domażlice
7. Horšovskýtýn

Fig. 3. Les Châteaux du type castel d'Europe Centrale, d'après T. Durdik, 1998B.

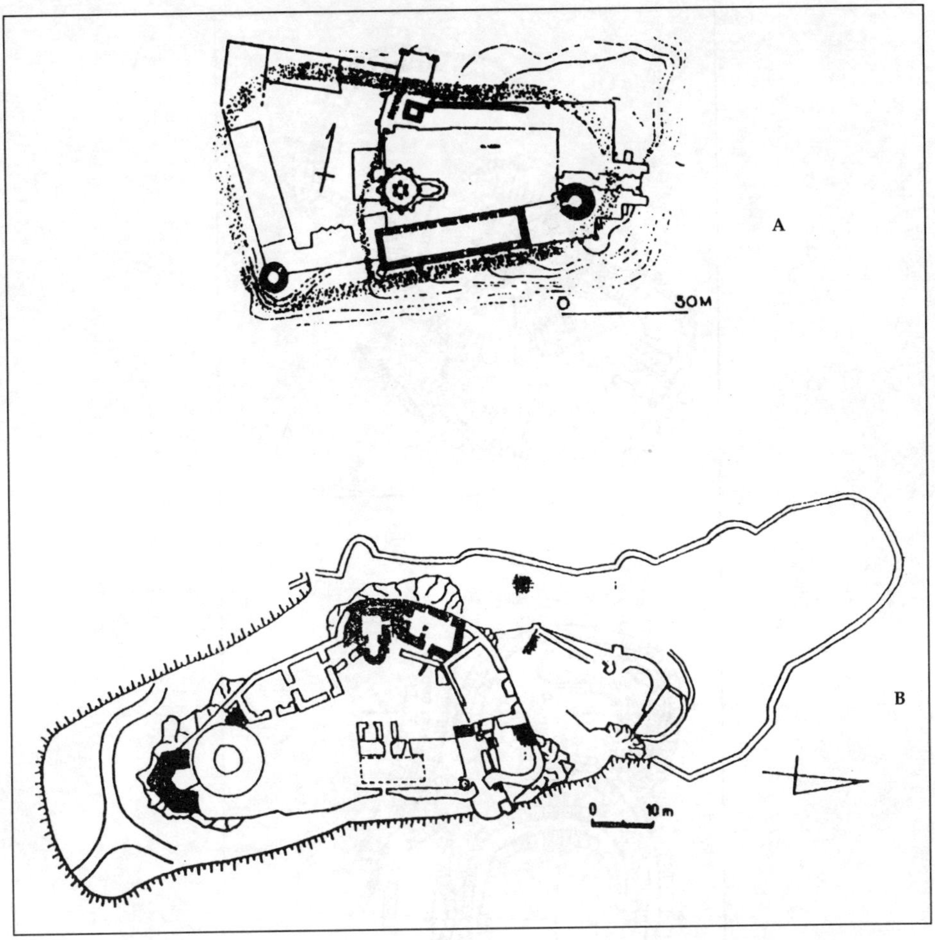

Fig. 4. Les Châteaux Romanes en Silésie, d'après A. Boguszewicz: A. Legnica, B. Wleń.

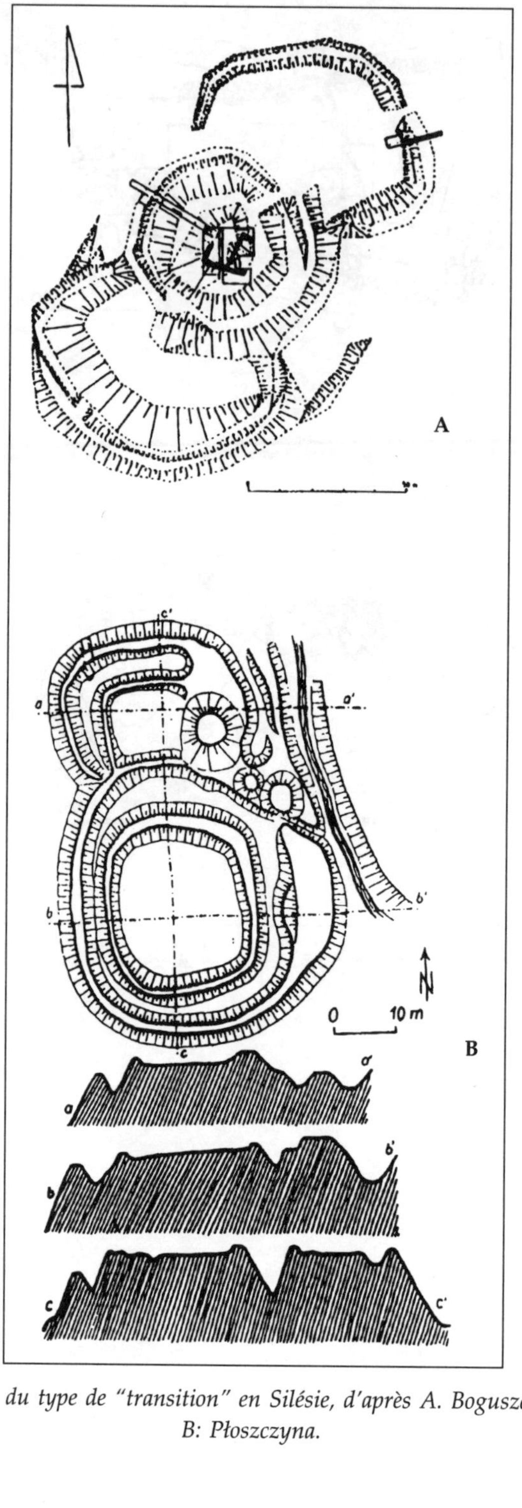

Fig. 5. Le Château du type de "transition" en Silésie, d'après A. Boguszewicz, A: Pieszyce, B: Płoszczyna.

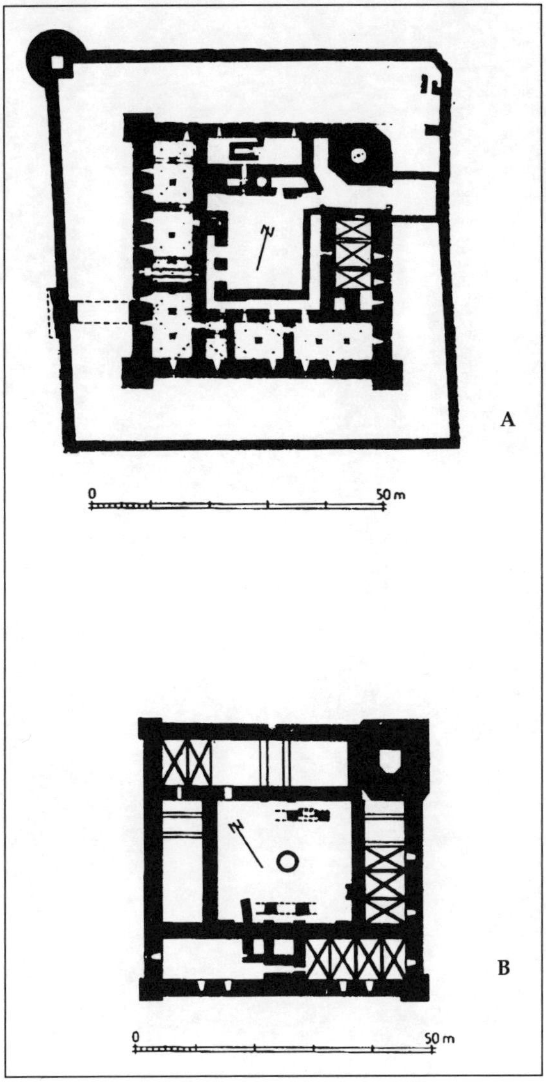

Fig. 6. Les Châteaux-Couvents des Chevaliers Teutoniques, d'aprés T. Torbus, A: Brodnica (Strasbourg), B: Gniew (Mewe).

THE DEVELOPMENT OF MEDIEVAL ARCHAEOLOGY IN EAST GERMANY SINCE 1990

GÜNTER MANGELSDORF
Greifswald

Some years ago, after the first meeting of the ESTMA, I have given a report about Medieval Archaeology in East Germany in the paper, which was edited by Hans Andersson in 1993[1]. Today with this review I intend to deliever an overview and certain new details about tendencies in Medieval Archaeology in East Germany since the reunification in 1990.

For most east-german people it was a great revolution of life and profession. This process of alteration in society and economy and also in science has not been completed yet. The whole system of science-management and nearly all institutions belonging to the Academy of Science in Berlin, universities and many museums fell down or were rebuilt. Many scientists lost their jobs, especially those, who were very closely connected with the communist party. The great Central Institute for Archaeology and Old History in Berlin was closed down and only a few colleagues have got a new job at the Römisch-Germanische Komission des Deutschen Archäologischen Institutes. All projects were stopped and research about slavonic archaeology came to a sudden end. The main newspapers, called Zeitschrift für Archäologie and Ausgrabungen und Funde came to an end too. Today there is only one paper left for all the east-german states, the Ethnographisch-Archäologische Zeitschrift. The Society of History of the former GDR with its department for Prehistory was disbanded. Also the Arbeitsgemeinschaft for Medieval Archaeology, founded in 1986, turned out to be fated to finish working and most of its members went over to the west-german Arbeitsgemeinschaft.

Politically the reunification meant a re-erection of the five eastern federal states, the so called Bundesstaaten; Saxonia, Thuringia, Saxonia-Anhalt, Brandenburg and Mecklenburg-Antepomerania. Each of them has its own Ministry of

1 Günter Mangelsdorf, "Zur Lage der Mittelalterarchäologie in der DDR", in Hans Andersson and Jes Wienberg (eds.), *The Study of Medieval Archaeology. European Symposium for Teachers of Medieval Archaeology. Lund June 11th-15th 1990. Lund Sudies in Medieval Archaeology,* 13, Stockholm, 1993, pp. 85-90.

Education, Culture and Science, which is responsible for all issues of culture, education, science and research. Furthermore there are different laws for universities, highschools and especially for excavations and the preservation of works of art in all these countries. For the purpose of supervising any action regarding preservation and research so called Landesämter für Bodendenkmalpflege with its directors, the Landesarchäologen, were installed. Because most of the great museums of archaeology have been undergoing a process of restructerizing their expositions as in Dresden, Halle, Potsdam and Schwerin are still closed. We have the same situation in regional museums too. Many archaeologists once employed at museums lost their jobs and departments for archaeology were widely closed, as it seems to be a question of money how much culture there is to be.

But what about the situation at the universities? Up to the end of the GDR studying our subject was only possible in Halle and Berlin. After the wall had come down new professorships for archaeology were established in Jena, Leipzig and in Greifswald. Most professors came from West Germany. Only at the Humboldt-University in Berlin and in Greifswald medieval archeology is a taught subject. Usually students only get a degree in prehistory, not in medieval archaeology. But in the last years many students finished their education with a final test in medieval archaeology and thus were awarded the magister artium. Since 1997 a new system of studying, with only 3 years of preparation and the BA degree like in other european countries, is under discussion at our universities. However our students do not like such short study periods thus most of them use to stay for five often up to seven years and finish with a doctor degree. Only some years after the "Wende" young archaeologists had a good chance to find a job. Although nearly all museums, institutes and offices are overcrowded today and possibilities to work within their profession are few, the number of students has been rising quickly since the reunification. Today there is a total number of about 1000 in Germany. Many of them like to go to a foreign country, best to North- or Westeurope after the end of their training. But I think it is very difficult to get a job there too.

Medieval archaeology has been becoming more and more popular during the last 10 years, also the opinion towards this subject changed completly. There are now strict rules or rather laws in each of the eastern german countries, which impose certain restrictions e.g. on investors. Before a house, a street or a factory can be constructed on historic ground, an excavation must have been carried out. Thus last years most investigations in East Germany took place in town centres, making this branch of archaeology the most paramout one. However, as the number of reconstruction sites decreases also excavations which are executed by the Landesämter in various towns,e.g. Leipzig, Dresden, Magdeburg Brandenburg, Rostock, Greifswald and Neubrandenburg, will become fewer. Beside this also regional museums as in Stralsund, Wismar and other smaller towns are involved to a certain extent. Anyway, about all these activities we have only short reports in several papers. One problem is that money is only granted for excavations, but not for a necesary documentation and publication of the gained material. Therefore the collections in several museums and in the Landesämter are terribly crammed with all kind of interesting artefacts, which have neither been published, nor been mentioned anywhere. Instead of field research, scientists are thus in danger of being forced to re-excavate these items in museums one day.

Although difficult to handle, did this flow of information show, that nearly all towns between Elbe an Oder were founded at the end of the 12th or at the beginning of the 13th century. Only a few towns in Saxonia-Anhalt and Thuringia turned out to be of older date. The cities in Saxonia, Brandenburg and Mecklenburg-Antepomerania have their roots in the slavonic period and usually came up near a slavonic castle or settlement with a commercial background. New in-town excavations illustrate the connection between slavonic and german settlements and the influence of material culture. With the german settlers came new forms of housebuilding to the area east of Elbe and Saale. The slavonic Blockhaus for example was soon replaced by the wooden Ständerhaus with a stone foundation. Slavonic material culture, especially pottery died in Brandenburg-Berlin in the late 12th century and in Mecklenburg-Antepomerania at the end of the 13th century[2].

Town excavations delievered new facts about handicraft in general and production techniques. Pottery kilns are known from many towns and new information about pottery distribution itself was gained. Articles about this branch were issued in Brandenburg and Thuringia. Only some years ago we did not know anything about medieval glas production. Now we have a wide spectrum of glass artefacts which were produced in Germany, Italy or Bohemia especially found in the rich hanseatic towns near the Baltic Sea. In Greifswald alone four enameled italian cups from the 13th or 14 th century could salvaged from the ground. A fifth was found in Stralsund[3].

All new details about the topography, the foundation, daily-life, trade, transport and craft give us a new impression of the medieval town in East Germany. Unfortunately the fruitful cooperation between historians and art historians hasn't been put into action. Not all of them accept the results of Medieval Archaeology in our Centre of Medieval Research –I have spoken about it in Budapest and Caen– historians and phililogists are dominating while the results of our studies are regarded far less important, at least that's what I think. What we need is an interdisciplinary alliance to cope with the different aspects of this issue.

2 Günter Mangelsdorf, "Zur Enddatierung der slawischen Sachkultur in Mecklenburg-Vorpommern", in Anke Wesse (ed.), *Studien zur Archäologie des Ostseeraumes. Festschrift für Michael Müller-Wille,* Neumünster, 1998, pp. 571-576.

3 Günter Mangelsdorf, "Glasbecher des späten 13. Jahrhunderts mit Emailbemalung aus Greifswald", in *Archäologisches Korrespondenzblatt,* 29, 1999, pp. 445-450; Cathrin und Heiko Schäfer, "Ein emailbemalter Glasbecher aus Greifswald, unter besonderer Berücksichtigung des Befundes und der Beifunde", in *Bodendenkmalpflege in Mecklenburg-Vorpommern, Jahrbuch,* 45, 1997 (1998), pp. 271-298; Gunnar Möller, "Ein goldemailbemalter Glasbecher des frühen 14. Jahrhunderts aus der Altstadt von Stralsund", in *Bodendenkmalpflege in Mecklenburg-Vorpommern, Jahrbuch,* 41, 1993 (1994), pp. 215-227.

New studies about villages, agriculture and the hinterland of towns have been very rare in East Germany for about ten years, because farming is still in an economic depression and financiers are pretty seldom. Formerly huge farms often declined totally or at least shrank tremendously. Often the unemployment rate reached 20% and more. Because only a few new-starters invest in buildings, there are virtually no excavations taking place. Thus, one of the main questions, concerning the contacts between slavonic and german settlements in the 12th century, is still left without definitive answer. How was the slavonic village constructed, what did it look like and what made german settlers come to the areas eastwards the river Elbe and Saale? Since the early 13th century new types of houses, new methods in agriculture and a new material culture are coming up there. Some years ago a new Centre for East-Middle-European History with a department called "Germania Slavica" was founded in Leipzig. Historians and archaeologists from this group researched in Saxonia, Brandenburg and in Mecklenburg-Antepomerania on these issues[4]. Nevertheless we need more excavations in medieval villages especially in deserted places, to gain new information. I hope a new project supported by the Volkswagen-Stiftung will be launched next year.

Other branches of medieval archaeology cover research on churches, monasteries and graves. Due to intensive coal-mining in Saxonia and in the southern part of Brandenburg for example many villages with their churches were devasted during the last ten years. Some churches were nearly completly excavated by medieval archaeologists and could with the help of the dendrochronolocical method be dated to be earlier then written documents conveyed[5]. The oldest churches in this landscape were founded in the late 12th or in the 13th century. Typical are buildings of stone –in Northeast Germany brick stones– with a rectangle room, a choir and an apsis. The gravefields are located around the churches. During the time of german colonization slavonic graveyards were closed and new churchyards were opened in the middle of the villages. Only one or two of such gravefields from the 12th up to the 13th century were excavated completly. In contrast to slavonic graves the german counterparts are without any supplements[6].

In the middle of the 90's we started two projects in Greifswald. The first one supported by the Deutsche Forschungsgemeinschaft dealt with the hinterland of the cistercian monastery Eldena near Greifswald during the high medieval time. Later on, I carried out two excavations in the remnants of the monastery-church, discovering some earthgraves. With our surveys we threw light on the earlist period of the church which had been founded by danish monks from Sealand at the end of the 12th century[7].

---

4 Christian Lübke (ed.), *Struktur und Wandel im Früh- und Hochmittelalter. Eine Bestandsaufnahme aktueller Forschungen zur Germania Slavica*, Stuttgart, 1998.

5 Judith Oexle (ed.), *Frühe Kirchen in Sachsen. Ergebnisse archäologischer und baugeschichtlicher Untersuchungen*, Stuttgart, 1994.

6 Henrike Hesse, "Zur Untersuchung des mittelalterlichen Gräberfeldes bei Rädel, Kr. Brandenburg, von 1984 bis 1987", in *Ausgrabungen und Funde*, 33, 1988, pp. 97-104.

7 Günter Mangelsdorf, "Neue Ausgrabungen in der Klosterruine von Eldena bei Greifswald", in *Greifswalder Mitteilungen*, 3, 1999, pp. 225-291.

The second project is situated on the island Usedom near the Baltic Sea. Not far from the little town of Usedom one of the first monasteries in Pomerania was founded by the duke of Pomerania in the middle of the 12th century. This monastery was very important for the early history of Pomerania and a couple of dukes are even burried within its walls. Although the monastery was transferred to another part of the island in the 14th century and the site decayed heavily, we succeded to detect its ruins by means of aerial photography. Later on, geo-electric and geo-magnetic measurements enabled geophysics to fix the subterrean ruins on the field itself. In summer 1997 we started our first campaign there and discovered the stone foundation of a building from the 12th century, which was erected over a christian skeletton gravefield. Indeed, this project is likely to continue for some years[8].

Obviously, new techniques like aerial photography and submarine investigation were introduced in institutes, after the Wende. Even at our institute we use new high-tec facilities as for example in Usedom or Eldena, but the vast majorty of capacities is used in the maritime part of archaeology. Thus a great deal of partly precious shipwrecks from the late and postmedieval time could be detected along the shoreline of the Baltic Sea. Some of them even attracted media and became quite popular, thus prompting the interest in archaeology in the whole country.

Yet there is a lot of work to do. For example research on medieval castles, where our gap of information is especially wide and the work of cataloguing has been neglected for years. Unfortunately great projects to bridge these gaps, and work on new theories are rather seldom or don't exist after all, because of the costs. Anyway, we are on the right track, and with the increasing popularity of medieval archaeology in public we have a good foundation for innovating future projects.

[8] Günter Mangelsdorf, "Kloster Grobe bei Usedom. Bericht über die Ergebnisse einer Ausgrabung", in *Greifswalder Mitteilungen*, 3, 1999, pp. 155-190; Gerald Peschel, "Detailprospektion zur Aufsuchung des Prämonstratenserklosters Grobe im Bereich des Priesterkamps südlich von Usedom", in *Greifswalder Mitteilungen*, 2, 1997, pp. 243-272.

FORM AND CONTENT IN PRE-ROMANESQUE ARCHITECTURE IN IRELAND

TADHG O'KEEFFE
University College Dublin

Irish churches and other ecclesiastical buildings of the pre-Romanesque period are probably less familiar to international scholars than the free-standing stone sculpture, liturgical metalwork and illuminated manuscripts which are roughly contemporary with them. The architecture of the early medieval (or, as many Irish scholars term it, "early Christian") Irish Church is of course intrinsically interesting, and the literature on it is quite extensive[1], but the buildings are perceived not to be particularly accomplished, technically or aesthetically, either in their own right or by comparison with works in other art-media[2]. Most astute students of Ireland's early medieval civilisation would realise that such comparisons are negated by the fact that the skills which were required of early medieval builders were different from those required of metalsmiths, sculptors and book-painters, but still it is difficult not to feel that churches far more elaborate than those which survive from the first Christian millennium would have been more appropriate in an insular Christian culture of such artistic and intellectual richness.

The formalist approaches taken implicitly and explicitly by many students of early medieval Irish churches have contributed in large measure to the perception of these buildings as works of fundamentally unadventurous patrons and masons. It may seem rather invidious to pick out a number of scholars from among the many who have written about Irish churches from this narrow perspective –and I should perhaps include myself among their number[3]– but some exemplification is necessary.

The figure of Harold Leask will loom large in any modern historiography. His synthesis of early medieval and Romanesque architecture in Ireland was published almost half-a century ago and is still probably the best-known publication in the field[4]. Far more heavily influenced by the work of Arthur Champ-

1 General surveys include Leask, 1955, Radford, 1977, and Harbison, 1982.

2 Hamlin, 1984, p. 126.

3 O'Keeffe, 1998.

4 Leask, 1955.

neys at the start of the twentieth century[5] than he conceded, Leask arranged his material typologically and chronologically, and in tracing a unilinear development of plans and superstructures from simple to complex, he argued that timber forms of architecture influenced the trajectory of this development. Missing from Leask's synthesis is an appraisal of function and context, which were probably the variables which most affected both the appearance of buildings and the formal development of "styles"; also missing from his work is a convincing explanation for why the builders of stone churches would make them whole or partial skeuomorphs –imitations– of timber buildings.

A categorisation of pre-Romanesque stone churches not dissimilar to that of Leask was offered by Peter Harbison in his brief review of the subject twenty years ago[6]. Although a little more sensitive to functional and contextual differentiation, he privileged the formalist approach to the study of this architecture by offering the following categorisation:

1. Rectangular oratories of the "Gallarus" type, built in the corbelling technique (see Plate 1).

2. Simple rectangular structures with upright walls, subdivided into two groups according to the type of roofing used: (a) with timber roofs covered with thatch or shingles, and (b), with stone roofs supported by a stone vault.

Plate 1. Gallarus Oratory, county Kerry.

[5] Champneys, 1910.
[6] Harbison, 1982.

3. Simple rectangular structures with upright walls, with the addition of *antae* (shallow, flat-ended projections of the side walls past the end walls of a church: see Plate 2), again sub-divided into two sub-groups according to the type of roofing used.

4. Churches consisting of a rectangular nave with contemporary but smaller chancel.

It is true that all pre-Romanesque stone churches in Ireland could be described as belonging within one of these categories, and to that extent Harbison's scheme fulfils a basic function of typology by providing us with what might be characterised as a "descriptive shorthand". But its benefits in that respect are far outweighed by an inherent danger: it continues to highlight those particular variables –shape, roofing, the presence or absence of *antae*– which Leask had regarded as significant in understanding church architecture without being able to demonstrate why they should be so regarded. Do we know for certain, for example, that the way a church was roofed carried meaning for patrons and was noticed by congregations? Can we be sure that the presence or absence of *antae* was more significant than the use of a lintel or a monolithic arch over an east window? And, when we speak about "significance", for whom are we speaking: the patrons and masons, the medieval congregations, or ourselves? Harbison's categorisation perpetuates a particular formalist reading of this architecture, but a four-fold categorisation based on floor area, or wall height, or on the type of stone used, would be just as effective as a "descriptive shorthand" and might even be closer to the way churches were viewed and understood by early medieval populations.

Plate 2. Tuamgraney church, county Clare.

Another example of this formalist perspective is Michael Hare's analysis of early medieval Irish architecture, made from what he describes as an Anglo-Saxon (or English) perspective[7]. It comes as no surprise to those familiar with the formal characteristics of ecclesiastical architecture in Ireland and her nearest neighbour that Hare found comparatively few similarities between the churches of the respective traditions, but many of his observations –for example, "the double-splayed form of window is not found in Ireland, nor is there anything analogous to the double belfry window so common in Anglo-Saxon towers", or "the rich architectural sculpture of Anglo-Saxon England is not to be found in Ireland"– lead to a question which he does not ask: why not? Put another way, are we witnessing here differences of fashion, of access to Continental sources, of wealth, of chronology, or of function? And should we *expect* to find formal similarities between Irish and Anglo-Saxon churches?

Our immediate challenge in approaching Ireland's early medieval ecclesiastical architecture is to guard against simple qualitative judgements of the buildings, and to allow instead that these simple churches might reflect deeply-embedded aesthetic and iconographic values, not an innate inability among Irish builders to create sophisticated architecture with aplomb; indeed, the great Round Towers suggest that they had the capacity, not otherwise apparent to us, to build daring structures. The key points are these: first, the more we juxtapose in our minds' eyes the great richness of the *arts mobiliers* with the great simplicity of the contemporary churches in early medieval Ireland the more we should consider that architectural simplicity to be a product of choice, and secondly, the more conservative these buildings seem to be in this juxtaposition, the more we must consider that conservatism to have been ideologically-charged.

MOS SCOTTORUM, MOS ROMANORUM

The two principal terms used by Irish writers and chroniclers of the early middle ages to describe churches were *dairthech* and *damliac,* signifying wooden churches (literally "oak-houses") and stone churches (literally "stone houses") respectively[8]; other materials were also used for church building, such as turf and woven twigs[9].

Bede made a distinction between a Roman and an Irish manner of church-building, remarking that Benedict Biscop, founder of the monastery of Wearmouth, went to Gaul for *cementarios qui lapideam sibi aecclesiam iuxta Romanorum quem semper amabat morem facerent,* masons who could build for him a stone church in the Roman manner which he always loved, whereas Finian, an Irish bishop, built a church at Lindisfarne, *more Scottorum non de lapide, sed de robore secto,* after the manner of the Irish, not of stone but of split oak. As Richard Gem has shown, the distinction between the technologies must be understood

[7] Hare, 1986.
[8] Manning, 2000.
[9] Warren, 1881, pp. 85-88; Radford, 1977, p. 1; Hamlin, 1984, p. 118.

as a metaphor for the divergent practices and observances of the Irish (or "Celtic") and English Churches[10].

References to examples of wooden churches are generally found earlier than references to stone churches, but both types of structure co-existed in the centuries either side of a.D.1000[11]. In the twelfth century St Malachy built a timber oratory, *opus scotticum, pulchrum satis,* Scottic (or Irish) work, not devoid of beauty, according to St Bernard in his *Vita* of St Malachy[12]. Moreover, a commentary on Brehon Law in the Book of Ballymote of *c.*1400[13] contains a reference to an *ollam* who is a master of "stone building and wood carpentering", suggesting that practitioners of the two crafts were sometimes one and the same. The contemporaneity of wooden and stone churches is also indicated in a manuscript, H 3 17 (Trinity College, Dublin), written in the central or later middle ages, which gives details of the payment for the construction of wooden and stone churches[14]. Finally, the palace built in 1172 to accommodate Henry II while in Dublin was built with posts and wattles[15]. Warwick Rodwell remarked that in the Anglo-Saxon world "stonemasonry was by far the lesser craft in the construction industry down to the end of the 11th century"[16]. The same might be true of early medieval Ireland.

We possess early medieval written descriptions –or, more accurately, descriptive accounts– of some wooden churches, and some of these suggest structures of considerable technical and aesthetic sophistication, as we will see below, but the examples of wooden churches which have been identified in archaeological excavations were clearly small, simple, post-built structures (Fig. 1).

The term *damliac* is first recorded in 725 as a place-name in county Meath (the modern recension is Duleek); the very fact that a place bore the name "stone church" suggests that churches of this material were unusual at this time[17]. The term was used by annalists more than forty times between the middle of the eighth century and the middle of the twelfth[18]. One of the earliest buildings described as a *damliac* was the "great church" at Clonmacnois, erected about 909, and this building still stands, albeit much altered[19]: it was originally of rectangular plan, 18.8 m by 10.7 m internally, with *antae* at its eastern and western ends, and it was entered from the west, probably through a lintelled doorway.

It should be noted, however, that this "great church" at Clonmacnois is a rare Irish instance of an historically-documented early medieval church being

---

10 Gem, 1983; see also Radford, 1977, Hamlin, 1982, and Harbison, 1984, for references to Bede's testimony.

11 Manning, 2000, Table 1.

12 Lawlor, 1920, p. 32.

13 Radford, 1977, p. 2.

14 Petrie, 1845, pp. 364-366.

15 Byrne, 1973, p. 52.

16 1986, p. 171.

17 Hamlin, 1984, p. 118.

18 Manning, 2000.

19 Manning, 1994.

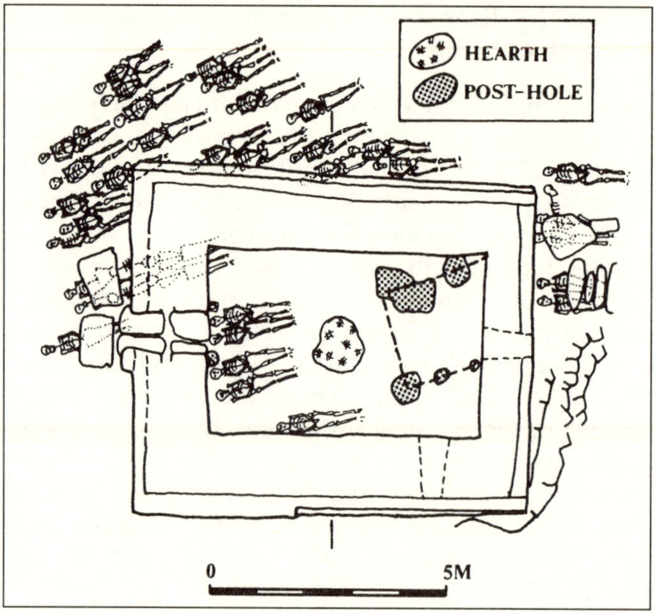

Fig. 1. Church Island, county Kerry, showing the remains of a wooden building and its associated cemetery beneath a stone church (see O'Kelly 1958).

identifiable with an extant building. The historical sources often record the existence, and sometimes also the construction or burning, of churches on many church sites, but it is rarely possible to equate those churches with buildings which still stand, in part because there was often more than one church on each site, and in part because there are occasionally multiple references to a church. Multiple references to conflagrations at monastic sites are equally frustrating because it is not always clear what was destroyed and what therefore needed rebuilding. St Feichín's church at Fore, county Westmeath, for example, bears clear evidence of having been destroyed by fire at some stage of its history but historical references to conflagrations at Fore are so numerous (they are recorded in a.D.771, 830, 870, 1025, 1069, 1095, 1112, 1114 and 1169[20]) and so vague (they do not always specify whether all or part of the site was affected) as to be of little value to the archaeologist; on architectural grounds the church is possibly tenth century in date, in which case its construction might not have been precipitated by the destruction of an older church. The development of a technique to date mortar by radiocarbon analysis offers a means of establishing the chronology of churches both independently and by calibration with historical sources, and some of the dates which have been produced are as one might expect[21].

Small stone-built "oratories" such as that at Gallarus, county Kerry (Plate 1), could perhaps be described as examples of *damliac,* but it is probable that the

---

20 Leask, n.d., pp. 4-5.
21 Berger, 1995.

annalists who used this word reserved it for buildings like the church at Clonmacnois: vertically-walled mortared buildings (though not necessarily with *antae)* which, like the words *domus* and *liacc* themselves, give a hint of *Romanitas;* in any case, Gallarus-type oratories are confined to the west (especially to the south-west) coast of Ireland, and they can be regarded, whatever their date, as examples of a local building tradition which had no obvious impact on architectural development elsewhere in Ireland[22].

Other terms used to refer to churches in early medieval Irish sources are *oratorium* and *teampall,* and possibly *cill.* Their use and most appropriate translations have been discussed by Manning[23]. One word which was in circulation in early medieval Ireland was *basilicum.* Its use indicates a church containing corporeal relics[24]. Although none survives, the Irish basilicas may have had their pedigree in the Constantinian and post-Constantinian practice of erecting basilical halls for the celebration of the mass directly above the burial-places of martyrs, thus forging a direct spatial and ritual relationship between the martyr's grave and the altar of the church above, while ensuring also a symbiosis of church and martyr-shrine in later architectural developments in the middle ages[25].

One term of particular interest is *erdam* (or *erdamh / airdamh).* Only half a dozen references to this feature are known, and they range in date from 825 to 1156[26]. Manning suggests that five of the six instances of its use indicate that it was a free-standing structure. Interpretations of its meaning vary. It was understood to be a "side-house, or [a structure] against a house externally" in the so-called Cormac's Glossary *(Senas Cormaic),* the dictionary of terms which was compiled by a bishop-king, Cormac Mac Cuillennain who died in 908[27]. George Petrie understood it to be the Irish equivalent of the Latin *porticus,* noting that the Irish translation of Bede's *porticum martyrii* from *De Locus Sanctis* was *irdum* in the fourteenth-century *Leabhar Breac*[28]. Radford also regarded *erdam* as equivalent to *porticus*[29]. In the context of Kells, where it was described as being the "western *erdam*", Hamlin interpreted it as a western "annexe"[30]; it was from here that the Book of Kells was stolen in 1007. Although I have interpreted *erdam* as a substantial structure projecting westwards of a church, rather like a *westwerk* in north Continental Europe[31], it might be better, in the absence of less ambiguous evidence in the annalistic sources, to understand *erdam* in terms of liturgical or sepulchral function rather than to regard it as a particular form of building.

---

22 For contrary views on the date and significance compare Harbison, 1970, and O'Keeffe, 1998.
23 Manning, 2000.
24 Doherty, 1984.
25 See Grabar, 1946, for the early medieval context.
26 Manning, 2000, p. 40.
27 Petrie, 1845, p. 438; Kenney, 1929, p. 11.
28 1845, p. 440.
29 1977, p. 4.
30 1984, p. 119.
31 O'Keeffe, 1996.

Paper buildings

Before examining the archaeological, as distinct from historical, evidence for stone churches, we must consider briefly two very important seventh-century descriptions of churches. The first is the timber "oratory" described in the poem *Hisperica Famina*[32]. The appropriate section is between lines 547 and 600 of an extant Latin text –the so-called "A-Text"– of the poem, and the following is Michael Herren's translation:

> This wooden oratory is fashioned out of candle-shaped beams;
> it has sides joined by four-fold fastenings;
> the square foundations of the said temple give it stability,
> from which springs a solid beamwork of massive enclosure;
> it has a vaulted roof above;
> square beams are places in the ornamented roof.
> It has a holy altar in the centre,
> on which the assembled priests celebrate the Mass.
> It has a single entrance from the western boundary,
> which is closed by a wooden door that seals the warmth.
> An assembly of planks comprises the extensive portico;
> there are four steeples at the top.
> The chapel contains innumerable objects,
> which I shall not attempt to unroll from my wheel of words.

Elsewhere in the same work –lines 62-63– is a brief reference to the tradition of building churches in wood:

> Do you hew the sacred oaks with axes,
> in order to fashion square chapels with thick beams

The closing lines of the principal section –the poet's admission that he will not try to describe what is inside the chapel– leads us to believe that it was the structure, not the contents, which was most remarkable. The details of the oratory have been analysed by Peter Harbison and, more recently and more comprehensively, by Niall Brady[33]. Although they do not state it explicity, both imagine the author of this remarkable passage standing in front of an actual building, wishing to describe it, and searching hard for appropriate words. They seem to regard the passage as reportage, as an objective a description as the author could manage.

One could query whether a building conforming to the description actually existed, but still interpret the passage as an attempt to render in words an impression of how a carpentered church of that period might have looked. However, a literal reading of the passage may not be what the poet expected of his audience. Neither Harbison nor Brady consider that the context of the descrip-

---

32 Herren, 1974.

33 Brady, 199x.

tion is a text rich in cosmological allusions[34]. One excerpt will suffice to demonstrate that motifs used in the "description" of the oratory are not exclusive to that particular passage:

> The throne of heaven supports throngs of angels,
> it forms the lofty vault with blue colour.
> Natural philosophers affirm that the heavenly cycle is sevenfold.
> Innumerable formations [of stars] stand at the top of the sky,
> which I shall not struggle to explain within the allotted time[35].

The author of the "description" of the oratory in *Hisperica Famina* should, perhaps, be regarded as its builder. I mean this metaphorically: he "built" the image of the oratory on his page by choosing his words as carefully as a carpenter might choose timber, and by arranging those words in a certain configuration, again just as a carpenter would. But I also mean it literally: what we see in this excerpt is a conscious construction of a metaphor of cosmological space, not an objective description which may conjure up a visual image of a particular church for those of us not privileged to see it in reality. A good parallel is provided by John Scottus Eriugena's poem, *Aulae Sidereae*, written for the dedication of Charles the Bald's new church at Compiègne, in which the structure of the church is clearly described as a Christological metaphor[36]. One further observation about the *Hisperica Famina* "oratory" is that its "builder", as we have styled the poet in this analysis, seems to have been at pains to let us know that it was not a stone church. This suggests that the *material* was a significant element within its iconographic intelligibility. We have already commented on the Bede's use of the iconography of materiality with respect to the Irish and Roman "manners" of building. It might be significant to note that some architectural forms of the Romanesque Church in Ireland, among them the portal of Clonfert Cathedral, county Galway (Plate 3) and the chancel of Monaincha church, county Tipperary, may be adaptations of timber architecture to stone.

The second description is that of the rebuilding of St Brigit's church in Kildare as recorded in the *Life of St Brigit* by Cogitosus, written in the first half of the seventh century.

> 32 Of the Church Door[37]
>
> 1. Neither should one pass over in silence the miracle wrought in the repairing of the church in which the glorious bodies of both –namely Archbishop Conleth and our most flourishing virgin Brigit– are laid on the right and left of the ornate altar and rest in tombs adorned with a refined profusion of gold, sil-

---

[34] Smyth, 1996.

[35] Smyth, 1996, pp. 89 and 115.

[36] Foussard, 1971.

[37] Connolly and Picard, 1987, pp. 25-26.

Plate 3. The portal of Clonfert Cathedral, county Galway; this may have been designed by a mason familiar with, or identending to imitate, a timber architectural form.

ver, gems and precious stones with gold and silver chandeliers hanging from above and different images presenting a variety of carvings and colours.

2. Thus, on account of the growing number of the faithful of both sexes, a new reality is born in an age-old setting, that is a church with its spacious sitet and its awesome height towering upwards. It is adorned with painted pictures and inside there are three chapels which are spacious and divided by board walls under the single roof of the cathedral church. The first of these walls, which is painted with pictures and covered with wall-hangings, stretches widthwise in the east part of the church from one wall to the other. In it are two doors, one at either end, and through the door situated on the right, one enters the sanctuary to the altar where the archbishop offers the lord's sacrifice together with his monastic chapter and those appointed to the sacred mysteries. Through the other door, situated on the left-side of the aforesaid cross-wall, only the abbess and her nuns

and faithful widows enter to partake of the banquet of the body and blood of Jesus Christ.

3. The second of these walls divides the floor of the building into two equal parts and stretches from the west wall to the wall running across the church. This church contains many windows and one finely wrought portal on the right side through which the priests and the faithful of the male sex enter the church, and a second portal on the left side through which the nuns and congregation of women faithful are accustomed to enter. And so, in one vast basilica, a large congregation of people of varying status, rank, sex and local origin, with partitions placed between them, prays to the omnipotent Master, differing in status, but one in spirit.

The description, for all its detail, does not tell us enough to know exactly how this church appeared externally, how it was roofed, or even (despite the near-universal assumption that it was of wood) what material was used in its construction. It was not, after all, Cogitosus's intention to allow us create an exact image in our minds' eyes. However, no commentator has doubted that the building described by Cogitosus actually stood at Kildare, and no objection to that consensus is raised here.

The description contains tantalising allusions to both architectural and social practices, and more specifically to the manner in which one was embedded in the other, and these deserve more detailed analysis than is possible here, but a few observations on how space was used within the building which Cogitosus described are germane to this discussion. The longitudinal division into two parts, one for males and the females, with the latter on the left-hand side (or north), is because this was the church of a double monastery and both sexes needed to be accommodated. The location of the sexes inside the building conformed to deeply-embedded tradition of gender placement, with females on the north / cold / left *–sinister–* side; it is interesting that the portal which features so prominently in the account was that serving the male community, even though the monastery had, in Brigit, a female saint. The opposed doorways in the church suggest that the two communities actually lived on different sides of the church. The two parts of the church's interior may effectively have constituted two churches under one roof, each with an altar containing the corporeal relics of a different sex; there are possible parallels here with the two near-contemporary basilicas at Armagh and with the location of churches relative to each other on many ecclesiastical sites[38]. This, combined with Cogitosus's description of an image-laden screen comparable with Benedict Biscop's *tabulatum* at Wearmouth[39], leads us to think of the Kildare church is being as close an architectural expression of *Romanitas* as we can detect in the built-environment of Ireland.

TOMB-CHURCHES AND THEIR ARCHITECTURAL INFLUENCE

Turning now to the archaeological evidence, the evidence of the few reliably dated pre-Romanesque stone churches, and of those churches which can

---

38 O'Keeffe, 1998, p. 118.

39 Meyvaert, 1979; O'Keeffe, 1998, p. 118.

be considered early medieval because Romanesque features and details have been inserted into them, allows us to isolate the characteristic features of Irish pre-Romanesque architectural traditions, and then to isolate a core of possible pre-Romanesque buildings from among the extensive corpus of undated Irish churches. Two traditions, broadly defined according to their technology, have already been mentioned: the first is comprised of dry-stone buildings, and Gallarus Oratory is the best-known example, and the second, which seems to be described by the word *damliac,* is comprised of mortared churches such as that at Clonmacnois. It is to that second tradition that we now return.

Prior to the eleventh century, the churches were apparently all single-celled and rectangular in plan. The smallest examples, such as *Teampall Dhiarmida* on the Lough Ree island of Inchcleraun (Plate 4) which measures only 2.50m by 2.10m internally, *Teach Chiaráin* at Clonmacnois which measures about 3.80m by 2.50m internally, and *Teach Molaise* on Inishmurray, county Sligo, which measures 2.7m by 2.4m internally, are best regarded as the tomb-churches of the saints who founded the monasteries in which they are located[40]. Radiocarbon-dating of their mortar indicates that these might actually be the oldest mortared buildings in Christian Ireland, and it is tempting to think that the genesis of the *damliac* –defined above as a stone church with vertical, mortared walls– lies

Plate 4. Teampall Dhiarmida, *Inchcleraun, Lough Ree.*

[40] Herity, 1993.

in this funerary architecture[41]. The fact that a number of these tomb-churches have *antae* may be very significant, as we will discuss below.

Leaving aside those buildings which are obviously tomb-churches, most of other early medieval churches in Ireland range in scale between, say, Killoughternane, county Carlow[42], which is 5.70m by 3.65m internally, and Tuamgraney and Fore in counties Clare and Westmeath respectively, each a little over 11m by 7m internally. The largest examples are Clonfert Cathedral, Clonmacnois Cathedral and Glendalough Cathedral, internally measuring 20m by 8.25m, 18.80m by 10.7m, and 14.75m by 9m respectively; none of these was of cathedral status until the reform of the Irish Church in the twelfth century. There appears to be a general relationship between the absolute size and relative proportions of the buildings: those less than 5m long appear not to have ratios of more than 1:1.5, while slightly larger churches with lengths of between 5m and 11m range between 1:1.4 (approximately the Vitruvian proportion of 1:√2) and 1:1.7 in their proportions.

The doorways of these churches are always in the west walls; the church described by Cogitosus at Kildare is the only pre-Romanesque church in which two doorways into the body of the church, neither of them in the west wall, are attested. Church portals in Ireland were lintelled prior to the late eleventh century; sometimes the lintel has a cross carved on it (Plate 5). The roofs were invariably of organic material, although slate may have been used where it was available: despite the claims of Leask[43], and more recently of the radiocarbon analysts[44], stone roofs are most likely to be of twelfth-century date. Every church has or had a single east window, either round-arched with a monolithic head, as at Killoughternane, mentioned above, or triangular-headed and formed of two stones, as at Kiltiernan, county Galway, Trinity Church at Glendalough, county Wicklow, and the smaller of two churches at Coole, county Cork. Temple Benen on Inishmore, the largest of the Aran Islands, has a single window which, because the church is oriented north-south, is in the side wall. A similar building might have been the *Cell trasna* listed in the later twelfth-century *Martyrology of Gorman* and explained in a gloss as "a transverse church, whose orientation is north and south, not east and west"[45]; its geographical location is not known to us.

Many of the Irish stone churches were not altered after they were built and so they remained small in size. In some cases, however, it was necessary to enlarge the area of a church, for reasons of liturgy or because of an increase in the size of congregation, and this was done in the eleventh century and later by the addition of a chancel. A number of newly-built churches of the late 1000s or early 1100s had chancels from the very beginning: Reefert (Plate 6) and Trin-

---

41 O'Keeffe, 1998, for dates.

42 Leask, 1943.

43 1955, pp. 27-36.

44 Berger, 1984.

45 Hamlin, 1984, p. 119.

Plate 5. The lintelled doorway at Fore, county Westmeath.

ity churches at Glendalough are probably the best-known examples. Prior to the eleventh century church-builders might have enlarged the sacred space by simply rebuilding their churches entirely rather than extending them. Such comparatively large early medieval buildings as the three future-cathedral churches of Clonfert, Clonmacnois and Glendalough, might not be the primary stone churches on their actual sites, but rebuildings of a date prior to the introduction of the concept of the chancel.

We turn, finally, to the *antae.* We noted above that these features are found on tomb-churches and on what we might be tempted to describe as "conventional" churches, by which we mean churches which provided environments in which the pastoral and sacramental needs of communities, either monastic or secular, were met. They are usually the only articulating features on the exteriors of pre-Romanesque façades and east walls. In virtually all pre-Romanesque

Plate 6. Reefert Church, Glendalough, county Wicklow, looking westwards from the chancel arch to the lintelled nave doorway.

examples the *antae* terminate with a horizontal stone course at the wall head; one pre-Romanesque exception to this is St MacDara's church on a small island in south-western Galway: here the *antae* turn at the corners of the two end walls and rise up the sides of the gables to the highest points (Plate 7). By framing both the end walls of churches *antae* emphasised the importance of these walls, one as the front of the church and the other as the wall behind the altar. Harold Leask, who was sensitive to the possible influence of the wooden architectural tradition on stone buildings and explored it as a central theme in his work, considered *antae* most likely to be "translations into stone of the corner posts of timber prototypes"[46]. None of those excavated structures in Ireland which have

---

[46] 1955, p. 56.

Plate 7. St MacDara's Island, county Galway.

been identified as wooden churches has yielded any evidence for wooden *antae;* one has to search outside Ireland to find possible examples of wooden churches with *antae*-like features[47]. The more pragmatic function which has sometime been suggested[48] is that *antae* supported the end timbers or barge boards of roofs. The combination of projecting *antae* and the overhanging roof would have created an effect similar to that achieved in stone by the builder of St MacDara's church. However, this function of the *anta* could just as easily be fulfilled by projecting corbels, as at Reefert in Glendalough, for example, even if it seems that such corbels were not have been used before the eleventh century –the suggested date of Reefert– whereas *antae* are used from the 900s. The presence of *antae* on the tiny tomb-churches must be regarded as very significant in our understanding these odd features. The tomb-churches are so small that the bulky *antae* almost overwhelm their façades and east-wall elevations, and this must be taken as an indication that these projections are not simple roof supports. We might consider instead the possibility that horizontal beams, themselves supporting crosses and other iconographic forms, were suspended on the tops of the *antae;* the crosses carved on the doorway lintels in some churches may reflect such a tradition (see Plate 5). The fact that the earliest examples are found on buildings containing corporeal relics may be an indication that later churches which are so adorned also contained relics. Is it stretching credulity too far to suggest that tomb-churches with *antae* were inspired by types of grave in which the long walls (the side walls) were simply sealed at

[47] O'Keeffe, 1991, p. 359.
[48] O'Keeffe, 1991, p. 359.

either end by closing stones? We might note that "slab-shrines", simple stone canopies over high-status graves in the early Church in western Ireland are essentially of this form[49], and that one might sometimes have been able to reach a corporeal relic by passing one's hand through one end of the structure.

SOME THOUGHTS FOR THE FUTURE

We take for granted today the concept of building a structure which is intended principally as a place of worship, whether we categorize it as a temple, a mosque or a church, or use some other label. But the process of conceiving a structure which is appropriate to a particular rite of worship is far more complex than the process of actual physical construction, and we deny its intellectual sophistication, even in the face of technical simplicity, at our peril. The collection of observations and reflections which forms the core of this paper is offered as a promotion of those methodologies which, as we know from the work of, among others, Carol Heitz[50], can be as sensitive to the *meaning* as to the *form* of architecture in the early middle ages.

As archaeologists we must underestimate our capacity to retrieve complex "meanings" in buildings. Eric Fernie, in an interesting analysis of the methodologies deployed by scholars in the study of medieval ecclesiastical architecture, has characterized the archaeologist's approach to the standing structures in terms of processes of recording and methods of period disentanglement[51]. None of us would dispute that the collection of morphological data, the establishment of chronology and sequence, and the representation of all that information in narrative and graphic forms which use universally-understood conventions, are necessary skills. We could argue, however, that Fernie's assessment does not do justice to our understanding of architecture as a complex expression and determinant of social identity, regardless of whether that architecture is regarded as ecclesiastical or secular. We could also argue that Fernie's assessment does an injustice to contemporary archaeology's interest in finding methods by which we can explore these subtle but significant functions and meanings of architecture. Krautheimer was probably correct in his thesis that the "content" of architecture was perhaps the key issue in medieval architectural theory[52]; conventional archaeological enquiry might not bring us towards content in the sense that Krautheimer meant it, but it does it allow us grapple with form, which is the medium through which and in which content is expressed and made intelligible. I do not intend this paper to be read an Irish version of those seminal studies by Krautheimer and Heitz, but I offer it as a tentative step in the direction of a more imaginative synthesis of early medieval Irish church architecture.

---

49 Thomas, 1971, pp. 141-142.
50 1986.
51 Fernie, 1988.
52 Krautheimer, 1942.

BIBLIOGRAPHY

BERGER, R. (1992): "14C dating mortar in Ireland", *Radiocarbon,* 34, pp. 880-889.

BRADY, N. (1997): "De Oratorio: *Hisperica Famina* and church building", *Peritia,* 11, pp. 327-335.

BYRNE, F.J. (1973): *Irish Kings and High Kings,* London.

CHAMPNEYS, A. (1910): *Irish Ecclesiastical Architecture,* London and Dublin.

CONNOLLY, S., PICARD, J.M. (1987): "Cogitosus: Life of Saint Brigit", *Journal of the Royal Society of Antiquaries of Ireland,* 117, pp. 5-27.

DOHERTY, C. (1984): "The basilica in early Ireland", *Peritia,* 3, pp. 303-315.

FERNIE, E. (1988): "Contrasts in the Methodology and Interpretation of Medieval ecclesiastical architecture", *Archaeological Journal,* 145, pp. 344-364.

FOUSSARD, M. (1971): "Aulae Siderae: vers de Jean Scot au Roi Charles", *Cahiers Archéologiques,* 21, pp. 79-88.

GEM, R. (1983): "Towards an iconography of Anglo-Saxon architecture", *Journal of the Warburg and Courtauld Institutes,* 46, pp. 1-18.

GRABAR, A. (1946): *Martyrium.* Paris.

HAMLIN, A. (1984): "The study of early Irish churches", in P. Ní Chatháin and M. Richter (eds.), *Ireland and Europe - the early Church,* Stuttgart, pp. 117-126.

HAMLIN, A. (1985): "The archaeology of the Irish Church in the eighth century", *Peritia,* 4, pp. 279-299.

HARBISON, P. (1970): "How old is Gallarus oratory? A reappraisal of its role in early Irish architecture", *Medieval Archaeology,* 14, pp. 34-59.

HARBISON, P. (1982): "Early Irish churches", in H. Löwe (ed.), *Die Iren und Europa im früheren Mittelalter,* Stuttgart, pp. 618-629.

HARE, M. (1986): "The study of early church architecture in Ireland: an Anglo-Saxon viewpoint", in L.A.S. Butler and R.K. Morris (eds.), *The Anglo-Saxon Church,* London, pp. 135-142.

HEITZ, C. (1986): "The iconography of architectural form", in L.A.S. Butler and R.K. Morris (eds.), *The Anglo-Saxon Church,* London, pp. 90-100.

HERITY, M. (1993): "The forms of the tomb-shrine of the founder saint in Ireland", in R.M. Spearman and J. Higgitt (eds.), *The Age of Migrating Ideas,* Stroud, pp. 188-195.

HERREN, M.W. (1984): *The Hisperica Famina I. The A-Text,* Toronto.

KENNEY, J.F. (1929): *The Sources for the Early History of Ireland: I, Ecclesiastical,* New York.

KRAUTHEIMER, R. (1942): "Introduction to an Iconography of Medieval Architecture", *Journal of the Warburg and Courtauld Institutes,* 5, pp. 1-33.

LAWLOR, H.J. (1920): *St Bernard of Clairvaux's Life of Malachy of Armagh,* London.

LEASK, H.G. (1955): *Irish Churches and Monastic Buildings. I. The Early Phases and the Romanesque,* Dundalk.

LEASK, H.G. (n.d.): *Fore, County Westmeath,* Dublin.

MANNING, C. (2000): "References to church buildings in the annals", in A. Smyth (ed.), *Seanchas. Studies in Early and Medieval Irish Archaeology, History and Literature in Honour of Francis J. Byrne,* Dublin, pp. 37-52.

O'KEEFFE, T. (1991): "La façade romane en Irlande", *Cahiers de Civilisation Médiévale,* 34, pp. 357-365.

O'KEEFFE, T. (1996): "The Romanesque portal of Clonfert cathedral and its iconography", in C. Bourke (ed.), *From the Isles of the North,* Belfast, pp. 261-269.

O'KEEFFE, T. (1998): "The architectural traditions of the early medieval Church in Munster", in J. Sheehan and M.A. Monk (eds.), *Early Medieval Munster,* Cork, pp. 112-124.

O'KELLY, M.J. (1958): "Church Island, near Valentia, Co. Kerry", *Proceedings of the Royal Irish Academy,* 59, pp. 57-136.

PETRIE, G. (1845): *The Round Towers of Ireland,* Dublin.

RADFORD, C.A.R. (1977): "The earliest Irish churches", *Ulster Journal of Archaeology,* 40, pp. 1-11.

RODWELL, W. (1986): "Anglo-Saxon church building: aspects of design and construction", in L.A.S. Butler and R.K. Morris (eds.), *The Anglo-Saxon Church,* London, pp. 156-175.

SMYTH, M. (1996): *Understanding the Universe in Seventh-Century Ireland,* Woodbridge.

THOMAS, C. (1971): *The Early Christian Archaeology of North Britain,* Oxford.

WARREN, W.W. (1881): *Ritual and Liturgy in the Celtic Church,* London.

THE EUROPEAN COMMUNITY BEFORE THE EU. FROM ROME TO THE ARCTIC IN THE MIDDLE AGES

KETH E. LIND
University of Tromsø

Ideas about a European community are part of a long historical tradition. Issues on co-operation and unity between different states in a European framework date at least back to the Middle Ages, as does the discussion about which land areas should belong to an integrated Europe. During the tenth and eleventh centuries, much of Scandinavia converted from the Norse to the Christian religion. Later in the Middle Ages, in the twelfth to fourteenth centuries, most of the northern coastal area of Northern Norway was also included in the European Christian community. Through Christianity, the Roman Catholic Church created the religious fundament for European universality in the Middle Ages. In Norway, the Roman Catholic Church also acted as an important driving force in the colonisation of the northernmost regions –all the way to the border between Norway and Russia.

"REPUBLICA CHRISTIANIA"

Today's European debate is in many ways coloured by previous thoughts and ideas. A pan-European consciousness emerged in the Middle Ages, but the groundwork for this had already been prepared in no less than four decisive events in the time from the fifth century b.C. to the fifth century a.D.; the growth of Greek culture in the Mediterranean countries, the creation of the Roman empire, the founding of the Catholic Church, and finally, Germanic tribes invading the Roman empire.Through the Catholic Church, Christianity created the religious basis for European universalism. In the fourth century a.D. Latin was elevated to the status as a common language for the Roman Catholic Church, and Rome was the centre of Western Christianity[1]. The dissociation from barbariens, non-Christian peoples strengthened the European unity. The Roman Catholic Church introduced the idea about European universality. "Republica Christiania" –the Christian society– became a denominator for Roman Catholic Europe[2].

1 Karlsson, 1996.
2 Karlsson, 1996.

Except for the Muslims in Spain and the Mediterranean countries, the whole of Southern and Western Europe had been Christianised before the transition to the second millennium. In Northern and Eastern Europe, however, there existed religions other than Christianity; with the Slavic, Finnish, Sami, and Nordic peoples. These regions did not belong to an integrated Europe, which at this time in history was synonymous with Western Christianity. During the tenth and eleventh centuries, much of Scandinavia had become integrated in the Roman Catholic European Middle Age system. At the same time, towards the end of the tenth century, Russia had been Christianised from Byzantium (Constantinople), and was thereby incorporated into the Orthodox Christianity. Throughout the European continent there was, starting at the end of the tenth century, a Christian border which, with only minor changes over the decades, looks the same today as early in the Middle Ages. Europe was constituted as the Latin Christianity. European identity developed in parallel with Roman Catholicism.

The Byzantin Orthodox areas, including Russia, were not part of this European community. The reasons for this were, in the case of Russia, complex. Instead of Latin, which was the Church language of the West, the Eastern region chose Church Slavic. This fact is of special importance. For various reasons the Classical elements were so to speak filtered away when the country converted to Orthodox faith and became part of the Byzantin cultural sphere[3].

ROME–NORTHERN NORWAY

In Norway the Middle Age is placed to the periode between 1030 and 1537 a.D. With the foundation of a Norwegian archbishopric in Nidaros (Fig. 1) in 1152-53, the fundament for a strong national organisation controlling spiritual issues and material resources had been laid down. The ties to Rome did however ensure that the Church in Norway still remained an integral part of the European Catholic tradition.

The Western cultural civilisation of the Middle Ages was thus closely connected with Christian Europe. But areas of Northern Norway belonged to barbarism –the uncharted beyond– until well into the Middle Ages. In connection with the incorporation of the Northern regions into the mediaeval European community, much of the academic focus has been on economic factors associated with the utilisation of raw materials and trade; such as fishing for selling at a market, and the production of dried fish, fur-and hide-trading etc.[4]. Research has to little extent focused on power –and factors of ideology. Thomas Wallerström[5] has, in his analysis of the Middle Age in Norrbotten (Northern Sweden), demonstrated that a change in ideology produced the impetus to crossing the border between civilisation and barbarism, and led to Swedish colonisation of the Northern Swedish regions, and that the Roman Catholic Church was the

3 Bodin, 2000.

4 Urbanczyk, 1992.

5 Wallerström, 1995.

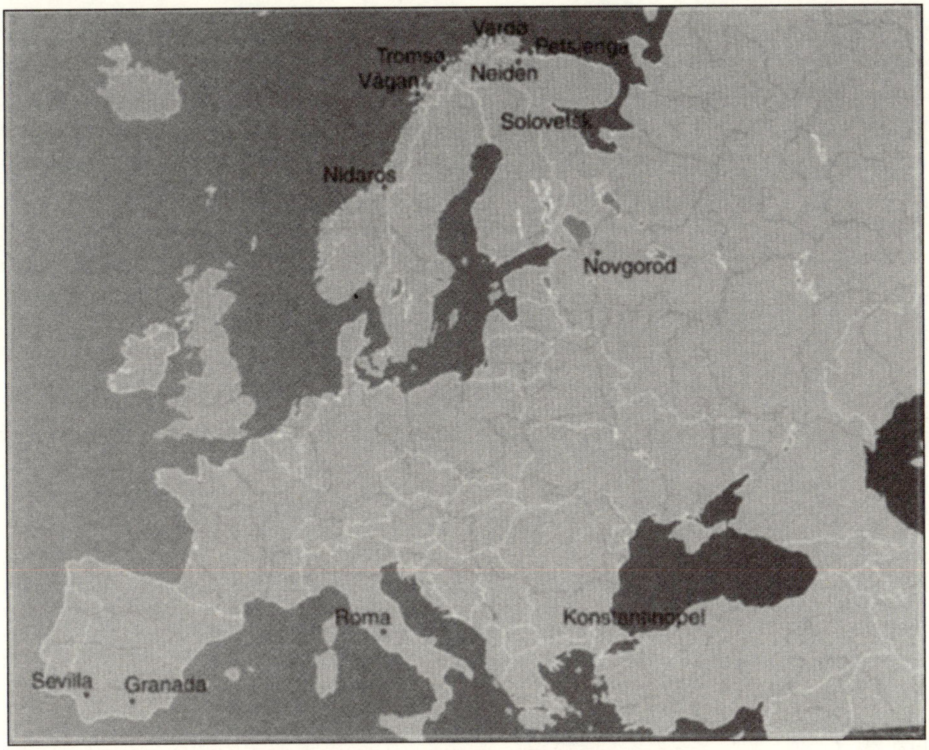

Fig. 1. Drawing Tromsø Museum.

driving force behind the colonisation. Lars Ivar Hansen[6] touches upon the same idea when claiming that the shift in power from local heathen chieftains to royal administrators and the Roman Catholic Church laid open the possibilities for Norse expansion into areas of Sami settlement. In this context, Norse should be seen as equivalent with the Norse peoples who first and in the largest numbers embraced Christianity, as opposed to the Sami population –and who are considered to make up the indigenous population in much of Northern Scandinavia.

From the introduction of Christianity in Norway early in the eleventh century until the activity of building churches had been introduced at Trondenes (Fig. 2), a relatively short period of time had passed. According to the sagas, King Øystein Magnusson (1103-1122) was the first church builder in Northern Norway. He allegedly built the churches at Vågan (Fig. 2) in Lofoten and at Trondenes. These so-called king-built churches were erected at the beginning of the twelfth century. As early as the eleventh century, however, Vågan was an important centre for the export of dried fish to Catholic Europe, and King as well as Church had from early on both economic and spiritual interests in the place. Reidar Bertelsen[7] emphasize that Vågan was placed in a traditionally

6 Hansen, 1990.
7 Bertelsen, 1995.

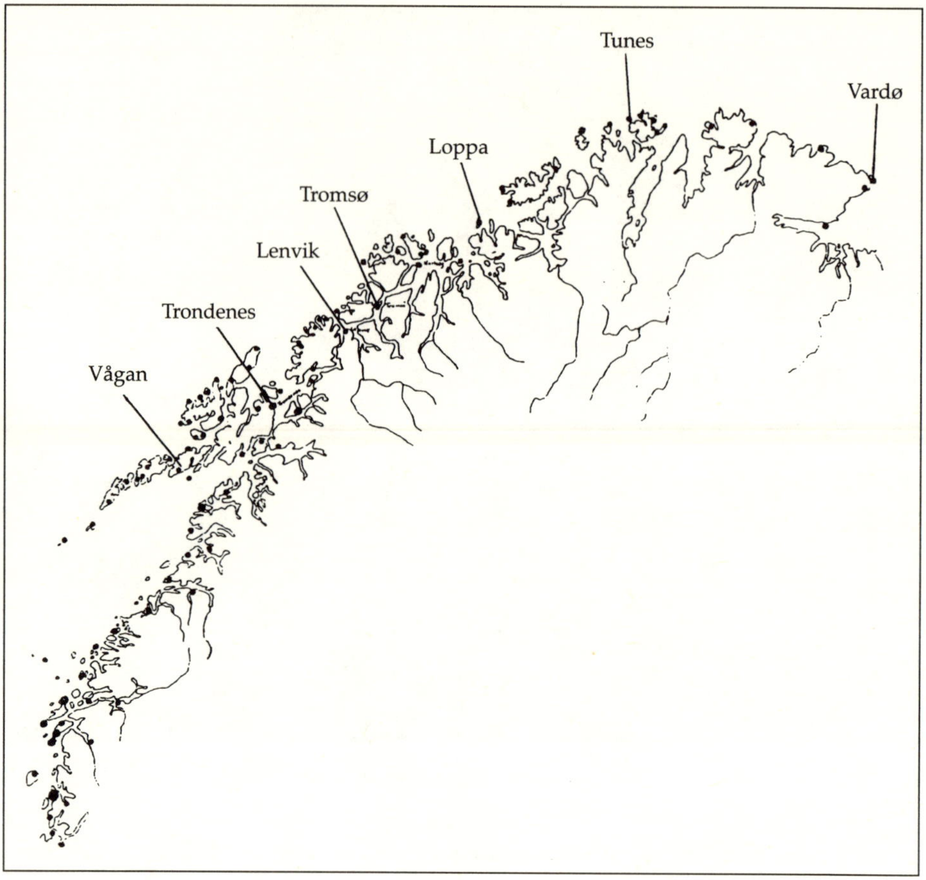

Fig. 2. Roman Catholic Churchers in Northen Norway in the Medieval periode. Churches mentioned by names occur in text or on picture.

Sami area of settlement. Norse settlements have long and strong roots in the surrounding areas, but when the centre Vågan was established, it was placed as a buffer against the Sami. Trondenes in the Iron Age (0-1000 a.D.) was a politicial focal point in Hålogaland. The place had a long tradition as a Norse and heathen centre of power, and bordered on Sami settlements. To have a church built at Trondenes was an important step for the Roman Catholic Church and the Latin Christianity. One may therefore assume that a church was built, possibly even the chieftain's private church, at Trondenes, before the reign of King Øystein, and perhaps even in the eleventh century.

Lenvik lies 75 kilometres north of Trondenes. According to the sagas, Lenvik was the northern boundary of Christianity and Norse settlement in the twelfth century. Moreover, few archaeological traces of Norse settlement in and around Lenvik in the Iron Age (0-1000 a.D.) have been found[8]. It is thus conceivable

[8] Gabrielsen, 1998.

that the Lenvik church in the twelfth century served as the Christian administrative northern border against the Sami region. There were, however, permanent Norse settlements, forming "pockets" in the Sami landscape north of Lenvik. The Norse settlements were spread along the outermost coastline as far north as Loppa Island (Figs. 2 and 3). Norse finds dating back to the Iron Age have been made in several locations north of Loppa Island, but it is not believed that these places had permanent settlements in the Iron Age; rather, the finds seem to be related to seasonal fishing and hunting grounds. The Norse settlement at Loppa Island appears to have vanished at the end of the Viking Age (approximately eleventh century). This population has either moved further south and into the Christian administrative area, or the Norse population has become assimilated; they have become Sami. Norse re-colonisation of Loppa Island does not happen until the end of the twelfth century/beginning of the thirteenth century[9], with the establishment of fishing villages and the establishment of a Roman Catholic church[10].

EUROPE'S SOUTHERN AND NORTHERN BORDERS IN THE MIDDLE AGES

In the thirteenth century, the Roman Catholic church reached the peak of its power. In 1248 the Latin Church expelled the Moors, Arab Muslims, from

Fig. 3. Ruin of Roman Catholic Church on Loppa Island. Photo: Keth E. Lind.

---

9 Bratrein, 1970.

10 Lind, 2000.

Seville in Southern Spain, and a few years previously also from Cordoba. The Muslim mosques, some dating back to the eighth century, were transformed to Roman Catholic churches. Muslim shrines were "Christianised" and "rendered harmless" with the aid of Christian symbols and Christian religious acts, and thereafter converted into churches and cathedrals. In my opinion, it may be interesting to point out that we find similarities in the way to deal with so-called heathen holy places in most of the Roman Catholic area, and we find "Christianizing" of the shrines and symbols of those having different religious beliefs also in Medieval Northern Norway. On the Sami sacrificial rock, the Troll rock, which today stands in the vicinity of the present-day church at Vagan in Lofoten, the image of a Christian cross had been scratched into the rock[11]. Thus, a Sami religious symbol was "rendered harmless" and converted to a symbol of Christianity. But, to concentrate our attention on Spain, apart from the sultanate of Granada, which succumbed to the Spanish as late as 1491, Southern Spain at the middle of the thirteenth century was the southern border of Roman Catholic Christianity as well as the European community, and faced both the Muslim world and, to some extent, also the Byzantine orthodox Christian culture complex.

At approximately the same time period as the Muslims had to abandon most of the Iberian peninsula, a royal Roman Catholic chapel was erected in Tromsø (Fig. 2), according to the Norwegian king Håkon Håkonsson saga. King Håkon Håkonsson's government was marked by much activity, both in its internal affairs as well as its relations abroad. For the sake of curiosity, it is worth noting that his daughter, Kristina, was married to a prince of Castile. At the middle of the thirteenth century, Tromsø was a cultural and political boundary marker for the Crown and Church, facing the Sami region to the north and east. At the same time, Tromsø formed a border relative to the competing political power in Novgorod (Fig. 1), Russia. Between 1250 and 1444, written sources document 11 attacks on Northern Norway from the Karel (Russia).

The Skansen fortification in Tromsø was probably built simultaneously with the establishment of the St. Mary`s church, signalling a secular demonstration of Norwegian supremacy in the region[12]. C-14 dating from Skansen indicates that the fortification was established in the period 1250 to 1300. In the thirteenth and fourteenth centuries, the boundary for Norwegian and Russian tax collection lay 100-150 km north of Tromsø. King Håkon Håkonsson negotiated a treaty with Novgorod which secured the peace in the region. Worth noting, however, is the fact that Tromsø in the middle of the thirteenth century also formed a boundary against a competing Christianity in spite of the fact that the Russian Orthodox Church was not physically established at the Norwegian-Russian border until the sixteenth century[13]. However, the Karel (Russian) invaders (from the thirteenth century), who incidentally should also be considered as regular tradesmen, were in addition representatives of the Orthodox Christianity. It is,

---

11 Bertelsen, 1995.

12 Lind, 2000.

13 Olsen, 2000.

moreover, interesting to note that even at the beginning of the sixteenth century, the Roman Catholic Church and the Orthodox Church did not recognise each other as Christian Churches; they mutually considered the other to be almost heathen. So: At the middle of the thirteenth century, the Tromsø region was the northern boundary of both Roman Catholic Christianity and the European community, facing the Sami, the princely power of Novgorod, and a perceived threat from the Russian Orthodox Church.

THE COLONISATION OF SAMI AREAS

The northern border was constantly, and also more rapidly, on the move from the thirteenth century onwards. It took relatively long from when a church had been established at Trondenes in the eleventh century until the border had moved north to Tromsø at the middle of the thirteenth century. When the church and fortification had been established in Tromsø, however, relatively little time passed until both the Crown and the Church marked their physical presence as far north as the border against the Russian area. Fortifications as well as a Roman Catholic church had been established in Vardø (Fig. 2) by 1307, and confirmed thus the Norwegian supremacy in the region[14].

It may appear that the treshold for invading a foreign border this late in the Middle Ages was lower than it had been earlier. Old traditions regarding the border between Norse and Sami areas gradually disintegrated, and at the same time it may have become increasingly pressing for both the Crown and the Roman Catholic Church to mark their presence in the region. In spite of the treaty with Novgorod, the perceived threat from the East seemed more alarming as the thirteenth century wore on.

It was predominantly the Norse population group in Northern Norway which converted to Christianity and gradually accepted Roman Catholic values, standards, world view and ideas. It was the Norse population group which, by its adherence to Christianity, became an integral part of "Republica Christiania", a part of Latin Europe. And it was the regions inhabited by the Norse population group which were first incorporated into geographical Europe. The areas north and east of this region, populated with Sami people, did not become part of this unity. It may be interesting to direct the attention for a moment to the relationship between the various peoples in Northern Norway. It may seem as if the core of our understanding of the relation between peoples in the Arctic regions today may be located in the social processes which took place in the Middle Ages, the Christian cultural tradition acting as a major contributory factor. In pre-historical times, we find mutual and equal relations between various population groups in the northern regions, Sami and Norse[15]. In the Middle Ages, new and different relations came into existence between the greater society/the central nation-defining element (the Norse) and what we today call

---

14 Lind, 2000.

15 Storli, 1985.

the indigenous population (the Sami). The greater society and the Christian European cultural tradition ended up in a superior position of power. The equality between the to peoples disappeared. Naturally, one cannot disregard the scientific interpretation of the world in the Age of Enlightenment (seventeenth to eighteenth century) when observing the state of affairs between different peoples today. The conviction in the Age of Enlightenment was that there existed a causal connection between physical characteristics and certain personality features, intellectual features or cultural features of different peoples, coupled with the view that certain peoples were innately superior to others. This view of mankind constitutes the very soil in which today's racism has germinated. Still, we cannot reject the processes which took place when the Roman Catholic church and the European cultural tradition took over the arena in the northern regions, as well as the fact that this has helped influence the relations between peoples populating the northern regions.

The majority of fishing villages along the outer coast of Northern Norway was established as permanent settlements in the thirteenth and fourteenth centuries, and have traditionally been seen in connection with the economic exploitation of the natural resource fish[16], which was in great demand in Catholic Europe in correlation with the Church's many periods of fast. However, I belive that in Nordland county, south of Troms and Finnmark counties, the fishing villages was established earlier. The establishment of fishing villages has, as part of a strategy of power politics, been absent from the debate. It has been assumed that the colonisation of the outer coast, through the establishment of fishing villages, was carried out by an already Christian population. For the Christians in the Middle Ages, church- and clergy-services were necessary to carry out the sacramental offerings, of which baptism and communion were regarded as the most significant and fundamental. The building of churches in the fishing villages has accordingly been directly connected with the local Christian population's need for church services, and to a far lesser extent connected with missionary work among the heathen (the Sami population). Active and purposeful missionary work concentrated on this particular people was allegedly not carried out until much later (seventeenth-eighteenth century).

We still cannot escape the fact that, second only to the necessity to render its services to a Christian population, the Roman Catholic Church was also a missionary church. The Sami, non-Christian population, which resided both in as well as near the fishing villages, would therefore be yet another important reason behind the desire to establish churches.

TO TAKE POSSESSION OF LANDSCAPE

In most fishing villages in Northern Norway, churches were built in the Middle Ages. Today, there are few and fragmentary written sources which can provide information about the Middle Age churches in Northern Norway. The

16 Urbanczyk, 1992; Bratrein, 1989; Holm Olsen, 1981.

source providing the best overview is Trondhjemske Reformats from 1589 (Inventery of landed property of the Church), consequently a post-Reformation source. It is still believed that the majority of the churches mentioned in this source, about 90 in total, date back to the Middle Ages. Only 10 of these Northern Norwegian medieval churches were built of stone in accordance with European building traditions; the northernmost was situated at Trondenes. The rest of the churches were built of turf/wood/stone. Today, many of these churches appear as ruins (Figs. 3 and 4), some also found in connection with churchyards surrounded by stone walls. As far as the church ruins may be interpreted, all the fishing village churches were constructed of turf, wood and stone in accordance with local medieval building traditions. The churches did not differ from the other buildings in any other way than being situated outside the cluster of buildings in the fishing village, having perhaps a cross on its roof, and quite likely being surrounded by the stone wall of the churchyard. The churchyard at Loppa Island had a pointed, elliptical standing stone marking each of its corners, something which served to further identify and distinguish the church and churchyard relative to the secular buildings of the fishing village. Architecturally speaking, the fishing village churches did not appear outlandish in the landscape. They were rather small, most of them measured 5 × 6 metres inside, and visually, the churches were not comparable with monumental structures such as e.g. the relatively large, thirteenth century stone church at Trondenes, which was constructed in accordance with European building tradition. But to their inhabitants, the fishing village churches must have seemed like monumental and holy buildings. The churches have served both

Fig. 4. Ruin of the Roman Catholic Church on Tunes. Photo: Keth E. Lind.

as representatives of a powerful ideological and economical power in the Middle Ages, as well as an expression of pan-European Christianity.

The fishing villages lie along the outer strip of the coast, all the fishing villages had churches, and there is more or less visual contact between the many villages. The mediaeval churches in the fishing villages had an unobstructed view towards the open sea. Most of the churches were clearly visible to people arriving in a village by boat. The fishing village colonisation and the construction of Roman Catholic churches have, as mentioned before, been explained from an economic market perspective as well as the need to provide services for a Christian population. The colonisers are said to have regarded it as essential to settle as close to fishing resources as possible; that is, on the outer side of the outmost island. Other explanations for why fishing villages and churches have been placed in such extreme parts of the landscape have not been discussed. We should not, however, overlook the possibility that the necessity for Church and Crown to demonstrate their supreme authority over the northern regions, became manifest in a form of choice of visible extreme points in the landscape. In this context, it becomes interesting to observe that the landing conditions for boats (small wooden boats) in many of these fishing villages are extremely difficult, even in good summer weather. In order to improve the landing conditions, and also achieve better protection from wind and weather for the settelment, the fishing villages would often only be required to move a few hundred metres. Moving the fishing village, however, would greatly reduce its visibility in the landscape, and the role of both the village and the church as symbols of the extremities of the landscape would have been lost.

CULTURAL INFLUENCE AND SEPARATION

The process of Roman Catholic Christian influence started in earnest when Christianity began to gain the upper hand on the Norse religion in the eleventh century. Erecting churches and chapels along the coast of Norway went quickly, first in the traditional Norse areas of settlement, and later also by establishing churches inside the colonised Sami areas in the thirteenth and fourteenth centuries. Both the missionary aspect and the need to mark a presence in the northern regions in a perspective of political, ideological and economic power, were important reasons for the Roman Catholic expansion.

In spite of the long and strong influence from the Roman Catholic Christianity, the various European nations had retained much of their distinctive national characteristics and their pre-Christian cultural heritage –and Norway was no different. But many of the pre-Christian customs, the ways of living and thinking, had been lost on the way. Christian rules and standards, which to a great extent had regulated the thoughts, actions and lives of people, had often been associated with force and sanctions from the Roman Catholic Church. A new way of living had impressed itself on people's consciousness.

The mediaeval Roman Catholic Church began to face major opposition at the beginning of the sixteenth century. The leader of what would become the disintegration of the Christian European community, was the Saxon monk and university teacher Martin Luther (1483-1546). Luther represented a religious and ecclesiastical re-orientation. In the 1520s, he rebelled against the traditional ideas of the Roman Catholic Church and the papal authority. In a few generations, many European countries severed their ties with Rome, abolished the Catholic cult and introduced the Lutheran Protestant Church. As far as Denmark-Norway is concerned, the Reformation was formally implemented in the autumn of 1536. The reason why it took until 1537 before Norway in reality had broken with the Roman Catholic community was, among other things, the result of a strong resistance against "Lutheran ideas", both from the clergy and the population in general. Those countries which converted to Protestantism in the sixteenth century, among them all the Nordic countries, broke away from the Roman Catholic hegemony, the Catholic cult and the papal authority.

The European community, "Republica Christiania", with Rome as its centre and the Pope as its religious leader, had disintegrated. At the transition to the Lutheran Church in the sixteenth century, however, several centuries of Catholic influence could not easily be erased. A mental (religious) and a physical/visual (churches and church art) community, founded on the Latin Christian doctrine, had in many ways tied people within the defined Europe together culturally. Much of the pan-European stock of ideas had been carried on into renaissance Europe. Also the Protestant Church in Norway had its basis and origin in the Roman Catholic heritage. But the centre of power itself had disappeared, and the control and influence no longer came from Rome.

CHURCHES IN THE NORTHERN NORWAY AND THE NORTHERN RUSSIA

No convents or monasteries were established in Northern Norway in the Middle Ages. The northernmost were found in the Nidaros region. In the northern reaches of Russia the situation was quite different. Between the fourteenth and sixteenth centuries, a number of Russian Orthodox monasteries and churches were established in Russia's northern wilderness[17]. Towards the border to Norway, however, no monasteries were established until the sixteenth century (Petsjenga 1533, Boris Gleb 1565 and Neiden 1565) (Fig. 1). Neiden lies on Norwegian territory, and the small Russian Orthodox chapel still stands there. The competition between the Roman Catholic Church and the Russian Orthodox Church in the Middle Ages was more a perceived threat than a real one. The Vardøhus church was the only church in the northernmost region for almost 150 years, but the threat that an Orthodox church might be established in Northern Russia must still have played a certain role in the establishment of the church in Vardø. It was the Lutheran Church, taking over for the Roman Catholic Church in 1537, which came into more direct competition with the Russian Orthodox Church.

---

17 Olsen, 2000.

THE CREATION OF A EUROPEAN PERIPHERY

In the past decade, people in today's Norway have become familiar with the term 'periphery'. The term has in many ways become synonymous with the northern regions of Europe, outside, far away and cold... But periphery requires an opposite –periphery must be relative to, and maybe also be dependent upon, a centre. The contacts, and particularly the trade contacts, which were established and maintained with the regions to the south in the Iron Age, were not based on centre –periphery relations. There existed no dependency between the North and the South. In the European consciousness, Northern Norway in pre-Christian times was an unexplored region inhabited by heathen barbarians. It therefore becomes meaningless to look upon the northern regions as European periphery *before* these regions had become incorporated into the Roman Catholic culture group. Northern Norway became a part of the European cultural sphere only when Church and Christianity were established in the region. The Pope was the central head of Roman Catholic Christianity. Rome was the centre of the Christian universe. Now, Northern Norway had a mental as well as a geographical centre to relate to. Northern Norway had become a periphery in the European Christian community.

BIBLIOGRAPHY

BERTELSEN, R. (1995): "Sentrale temaer i nordnorsk mellomalderarkeologi", in R. Bertelsen (ed.), *Om de første kirkene i Vågan og på Trondenes,* Universitetet i Tromsø.

BERTELSEN, R. (1995): "Sentrale temaer i nordnorsk mellomalderarkeologi", in R. Bertelen (ed.), *Borg og Vågan, sentra i hvert sitt årtusen,* Universitetet i Tromsø.

BODIN, P.A. (2000): *Ryssland. Idèer och identiteter,* Norma Bokförlag, Sverige.

BRATREIN, H.D. (1989): *Karlsøy og Helgøy Bygdebok, Vol. I, Fra steinalder til år 1700,* Hansnes.

BRATREIN, H.D. (1970): "Befolkningsforhold og kirkebygging nord for Malangen i eldre middelalder", *Håløygminne,* hefte 2-3.

OLSEN, H. (2000): *Den østlige pilegrimsvei. Oppbrudd og vandring i russisk-ortodoks tradisjon,* Verbum Forlag.

KARLSSON, I. (1996): *Europa och folken. En europeisk nation eller nationernas Europa?,* Wahlström & Widstrand.

LIND, K.E. (2000): "Det europeiske fellesskapet før EU. Fra Roma til Nord-Norge i mellomalderen", *Ottar,* 1.

LIND, K.E. (2000): "Tromsøboka, den andre", in Christensen et. al. (eds.), *Den gamle borgen Skansen,* Tromsøboka AS.

HOLM OLSEN, I.M. (1981): "Economy and Settlement pattern 1350-1600 a.D. Based on Evidence from Farm Mounds", *Nowegian Archaeological Review,* Vol. 14, n° 2.

STORLI, I. (1985): *Håløyghøvdinger. Om grunnlaget for og vedlikeholdet av høvdingmakt i jernalderen, med vekt på Sør-Salten,* Magistergrad i arkeologi, Universitetet i Tromsø.

URBANCZYK, P. (1992): *Medieval Arctic Norway,* Institute of the History of Material Culture, Polish Academy of Sciences, Warsawa.

WALLERSTRöM, T. (1995): *Norrbotten, Sverige och medeltiden. Problem kring makt och bosätting i en europeisk periferi,* Lund.

III

Specific Research Projets

MÉTHODE DE RECHERCHE ARCHÉOLOGIQUE SUR LES CHÂTEAUX DE TERRE ET DE BOIS. L'EXEMPLE DE LA NORMANDIE

Anne-Marie Flambard Héricher
Université de Rouen

Concernant les châteaux de terre et de bois, domaine où les textes sont peu nombreux ou peu explicites, et où les vestiges conservés sont toujours très lacunaires puisque les édifices anciens ont disparu, l'archéologie, et la méthode de recherche qu'elle induit, sont primordiales. C'est pourquoi il est indispensable, pour obtenir des résultats significatifs, d'effectuer la meilleure sélection possible parmi les sites à fouiller et ensuite, dans la mesure où une fouille totalement exhaustive est impossible, de bien choisir, sur le terrain, les emplacements susceptibles de livrer le maximum d'informations sur la fortification. C'est pourquoi la fouille d'un site castral de terre répond à une démarche qui ne souffre guère de modification; je l'évoquerai en suivant son déroulement chronologique en trois temps: d'abord le recensement des sites, puis la sélection d'un site en vue de le fouiller, enfin la réalisation de sondages suivis de la fouille. Nous évoquerons parallèlement les résultats attendus. Pour illustrer cette présentation nous nous appuierons sur des exemples normands qui, à des titres divers, ont constitué des étapes décisives dans l'élaboration de cette méthodologie.

PREMIER TEMPS: LE RECENSEMENT

C'est à l'initiative de Michel de Boüard que la recherche sur les fortifications de terre médiévales s'est développée en France. Elle a débuté dans les années soixante et tout naturellement, en Normandie, où il enseignait et avait créé le Centre de Recherches Archéologiques Médiévales (CRAM[1]). C'est à son initiative que les premiers recensements ont été opérés. Ils ont débouché sur quelques publications pionnières comme, en 1964, le travail qu'il avait lui-même consacré aux petites enceintes circulaires d'origine médiévale en Normandie[2].

---

[1] Le CRAM est devenu en 1999 le CRAHM (Centre de Recherches Archéologiques et Historiques Médiévales).

[2] Boüard de M., "Les petites enceintes circulaires d'origine médiévale en Normandie", *Château Gaillard I, Études de castellologie européenne,* Caen, 1964, pp. 23-35.

Il a été suivi, en 1968, par la thèse de Michel Fixot consacrée *aux Fortifications de terre et aux origines féodales dans le Cinglais*[3] puis par les travaux de Jacques Le Maho sur *L'apparition des seigneuries châtelaines dans le Grand-Caux à l'époque ducale*[4] et de Florence Delacampagne sur les *Seigneurs, fiefs et mottes du Cotentin*[5] qui furent respectivement publiés en 1976 et 1982. Très vite ces recensements se doublèrent de fouilles sur des sites sélectionnés: les études du Grand Beyle de Buchy[6], d'Urville et de Bretteville sur-Laize[7], de Rubercy[8], d'Audrieu[9], de Sébécourt[10], du Plessis-Grimoult[11], de Grimbosq[12] furent suivies dans les années quatre-vingt par celles de Mirville[13], de Notre-Dame-de-Gravenchon[14], de Saint-Vaast-sur-Seulles[15], et, dans les années 90, de Vatteville-la-Rue[16], de Ri-

---

[3] M. Fixot, *Les fortifications de terre et les origines féodales dans le Cinglais*, Caen, 1968.

[4] J. Le Maho, "L'apparition des seigneuries châtelaines dans le Grand-Caux à l'époque ducale", *Archéologie Médiévale*, VI, 1976, pp. 5-148.

[5] F. Delacampagne, "Seigneurs, fiefs et mottes du Cotentin (X[e]-XIIe siècles). Étude historique et topographique", *Archéologie Médiévale*, XII, 1982, pp. 175-207.

[6] H. Arbmann, "Fortifications autour de Buchy", *Meddelanden fran Lunds Universitets Historiska Museum*, 1968, pp. 41-84.

[7] J. Decaëns, "Les enceints d'Urville et de Bretteville-sur-Laize (Calvados), contribution archéologique aux recherches sur l'habitat fortifié", *Annales de Normandie*, 18e année, n° 4, 1968, pp. 311-375.

[8] "Rubercy, Calvados", Chronique des fouilles, *Archéologie Médiévale*, *III-IV*, 1973, pp. 410-411; C. Lorren, "La demeure seigneuriale de Rubercy", *Château Gaillard*, *VIII*, *Études de castellologie européenne*, Caen, 1977a, pp. 185-192 et "Le château de Rubercy, étude de la demeure principale (c. 1150-1204)", *Archéologie Médiévale*, VII, 1977b, pp. 109-178.

[9] A. Renoux, "L'enceinte fortifiée d'Audrieu (Calvados)", *Archéologie Médiévale*, *II*, 1972, pp. 1-88.

[10] "Sébécourt, Eure", Chronique des fouilles, *Archéologie Médiévale*, *II*, 1972, pp. 397-308 et *Archéologie Médiévale*, *III-IV*, 1973-1974, pp 411-413; J. Decaëns, "L'enceinte fortifiée de Sébécourt (Eure)", *Château Gaillard*, *VII*, *Études de castellologie européenne*, Caen, 1975, pp. 49-60 et J. Decaëns, J. Le Maho, "Recherches sur le site de l'enceinte fortifiée de Sébécourt (Eure)", *Trésors archéologiques de la Haute Normandie*, Rouen, 1980.

[11] E. Zadora Rio, "L'enceinte fortifiée du Plessis-Grimoult (Calvados). Contribution à l'étude historique et archéologique de l'habitat seigneurial au XIe siècle", *Archéologie Médiévale*, *III-IV*, 1973-1974, pp. 111-243.

[12] J. Decaëns, "La motte d'Olivet à Grimbosq (Calvados), résidence seigneuriale du XIe siècle", *Archéologie Médiévale*, XI, 1981, pp. 167-201.

[13] J. Le Maho, "De la *curtis* au château, l'exemple du Pays de Caux", *Château Gaillard*, *VIII*, *Études de castellologie médiévale*, Actes du colloque de Bad Muenstereifel (RFA), Caen, 1977, pp. 171-183 et *La motte seigneuriale de Mirville (XIe-XIIe s.)*, Rouen, 1984; voir également à ce sujet P. Halbout et J. Le Maho (dirs.), *Aspects de la construction de bois en Normandie du Ier au XIVe siècle*, Caen, 1984.

[14] J. Le Maho, "Notre-Dame-de-Gravenchon", in AV, *De la Gaule à la Normandie, 2000 ans d'histoire-30 ans d'archéologie*, 1990, pp. 173-176 et 194-195 ainsi que P. Halbout et J. Le Maho (dirs.), *op. cit.*, 1984; J. Le Maho, "De l'Antiquité à la fin du Moyen Âge", in J.-M. Cahagne (dir.), *Notre-Dame-de-Gravenchon, deux mille ans d'histoire*, 2000, pp. 23-69 et plus particulièrement, pp. 32-69.

[15] J. Burnouf et J. Decaëns, "La fin du château de Saint-Vaast-sur-Seulles", *Château Gaillard*, *XII*, *Études de castellologie médiévale*, Actes du colloque de Oostduinkerke et de Floreffe (B), 1985, pp. 23-37; J. Decaëns, "Les origines du village et du château de Saint-Vaast-sur-Seulles (Calvados)", *Anglo-Norman Studies*, X, 1988, pp. 83-100.

[16] A.-M. Flambard Héricher, "Premiers résultats des fouilles du château de Vatteville-la-Rue (Seine Maritime)", *Château Gaillard*, *XVII*, *Études de castellologie médiévale*, Actes du colloque d'Abergavenny (GB), Caen, 1996, pp. 85-89; *Id.*, "La construction dans la Basse vallée de la Seine, l'exemple du château de Vatteville-la-Rue",*Château Gaillard*, *XVII*, *Études de castellologie médiévale*, Actes du colloque de Gillelije (DK), Caen, 1998, pp. 93-102; *Id.*, "La cuisine du logis seigneurial du 'Vieux château' de Vatteville-la-Rue (Seine-Maritime)", *Autour du château médiéval*, Mémoires et documents n° 1, Société

vray[17], et de Bretoncelles[18]. Entre temps, en 1980, à l'occasion de la célébration de son 25e anniversaire et pour effectuer un premier bilan de cette enquête, le Centre de Recherches Archéologiques Médiévales de Caen organisait un colloque portant sur *Les fortifications de terre en Europe occidentale du* x*e au* xii*e siècle.* La prise de conscience de la nécessité d'un recensement méthodique des fortifications de terre peut être tenue pour une conséquence du colloque de Caen[19] qui a fortement contribué à en donner l'impulsion, particulièrement dans des régions jusqu'alors peu concernées par cette recherche.

Dès 1981, le mouvement était relayé et s'amplifiait avec l'initiative conduite par J.-M. Pesez (directeur d'études à l'École des Hautes Études en Sciences Sociales), et soutenue par le Conseil Supérieur de la Recherche Archéologique (dépendant du Ministère de la Culture). Une vaste enquête était lancée visant à élaborer, au niveau national, un inventaire reposant sur la mise au point d'une fiche descriptive normalisée des fortifications de terre. L'objectif final de l'entreprise était d'opérer un recensement sur l'ensemble de la France. Cette fiche descriptive était complétée d'un lexique visant à harmoniser la terminologie utilisée. Des relevés systématiques devaient compléter cette fiche: une échelle commune était préconisée pour les plans et une méthodologie mise à l'étude.

Cette initiative connut un début d'application dans quelques régions pilotes, celles où existait déjà une équipe d'archéologues motivés et sensibilisés à la problématique des fortifications de terre. La Normandie, avec le CRAM, se trouvait parmi ces régions. En 1982, 1983 et 1984, la fiche fut expérimentée. Une première exploitation informatisée fut tentée en 1984 et un projet collectif sur les mottes, les enceintes et les maisons fortes du Moyen Âge fut lancé[20]. Ce recensement détaillé prit de l'ampleur jusqu'à comporter 89 sites. Ensuite le mouvement se ralentit et, faute de crédits –car ce travail demandait des moyens conséquents sur une longue durée– la mise en œuvre de ce recensement détaillé et exigeant fut mise en sommeil. Lors du colloque de castellologie médiévale *Château Gaillard* xii, qui se tenait en Belgique, J.-M. Pesez a retracé la genèse de ce recensement[21], par la suite les Services Régionaux de l'Archéologie[22]

---

historique et Archéologique de l'Orne, 1998b, pp. 131-145; *Id.*, "Le *shell keep* de Vatteville-la-Rue (Seine-Maritime)", *Les relations entre la Haute-Normandie et le sud de l'Angleterre, Proximus,* ii, Rouen, 1998c, pp. 169-177.

17 J. Decaëns, "La motte de Rivray à Condé-sur-Huisne", *Cahiers Percherons,* 4, 1992, pp. 16-45 et *Id.*, "La motte de Rivray à Condé-sur-Huisne (Orne): de la motte de conquête (xie s.) au donjon seigneurial (xiie s.)", *Château Gaillard,* xvi, *Études de castellologie médiévale,* Actes du colloque de Luxembourg (L), Caen, 1994, pp. 109-120.

18 A.-M. Flambard Héricher, Ph. Bernouis et J. Decaëns, "La 'Butte du Château' à Bretoncelles, Un exemple de la conquête territoriale des Rotrou", *Château Gaillard,* xix, *Études de castellologie médiévale,* Actes du colloque de Graz, 2000, pp. 75-82.

19 "Les fortifications de terre en Europe occidentale du xe au xiie siècles", *Archéologie Médiévale,* xi, Caen, 1981, pp. 5-123 et particulièrement p. 123.

20 Cf. Juillet, *Projet collectif sur les mottes, enceintes et maisons fortes du Moyen Âge. Lexique. Système descriptif des fortifications de terre,* Conseil supérieur de la Recherche Archéologique, programme H 40, 1984.

21 J.-M. Pesez, "Approches méthodologiques d'un recensement des fortifications de terre médiévales en France", *Château Gaillard,* xii, *Études de castellologie médiévale,* Actes du colloque de Oostduinkerke et de Floreffe (B), 1985, pp. 79-90.

favorisèrent les enquêtes sur les fortifications de terre sans qu'aucune région ne parvienne à l'exhaustivité. En Normandie même, région qui était pourtant particulièrement sensibilisée à cette recherche, le mouvement se ralentit peu à peu. Dans le Calvados, le Service Départemental d'Archéologie[23] réalisa un inventaire local des fortifications de terre; l'inventaire global des fortifications de terre de l'Orne, puis celui de la Manche furent également mis en chantier mais ne sont pas encore parvenus à l'exhaustivité.

Dans le Bilan de la recherche archéologique en France de 1985 à 1989[24], publié en 1990, le Conseil Supérieur de la Recherche Archéologique soulignait la nécessité de procéder au repérage des fortifications de terre particulièrement menacées et depuis peu l'initiative ministérielle de mise en place de la 'carte archéologique' qui vise à recenser les sites pour mieux assurer leur protection a pris le relais des enquêtes d'origine universitaire.

2ÈME TEMPS: LE CHOIX D'UN SITE DE FOUILLE

Peu de temps après que les premiers recensements aient été opérés, et en s'appuyant sur les données déjà collectées, des fouilles se développaient en Normandie, aussi bien Haute que Basse, sous la conduite d'élèves de Michel de Boüard. Joseph Decaëns étudiait successivement Urville et Bretteville-sur-Laize, Sébécourt, la motte d'Olivet à Grimbosq, Saint-Vaast-sur- Seulles, Rivray et débutait l'étude de la motte de Bretoncelles, Claude Lorren fouillait Rubercy, Annie Renoux: Audrieu, Elisabeth Zadora Rio: Le Plessis-Grimoult, Jacques Le Maho: Mirville puis Notre-Dame de Gravenchon en Seine-Maritime. Actuellement, la dynamique s'est ralentie mais le mouvement se poursuit cependant tant en Normandie qu'en dehors de la Normandie où les enquêtes de Michel de Boüard et celles de ses disciples ont fait des émules.

Les différentes études qui viennent d'être énumérées permettent de construire une méthodologie de la recherche. Le choix du site, la manière de conduire les travaux, dépendent en effet des questions que l'on se pose et que l'on cherche à résoudre et de la problématique générale relative aux fortifications de terre. L'ensemble de ces interrogations permet de dresser une première liste de sites que leur potentiel rend susceptibles d'y répondre.

Ce choix dépend aussi du contexte historique local et des problèmes soulevés par l'histoire du site replacée dans l'histoire de la région. Ce second niveau de la problématique amène à dresser une seconde liste de questions, spécifique à chaque site, mais où l'on constate que certaines interrogations, redondantes, conduisent à aborder des problèmes récurrents qui apparaissent dès lors, du fait de leur répétition systématique, comme des problèmes généraux

---

22 Instance régionales dépendant du Ministère de la Culture.

23 Service dépendant du Conseil Général du département du Calvados

24 *La recherche archéologique en France 1985-1989,* Ministère de la culture de la communication des grands travaux et du bicentenaire, Direction du patrimoine, sous-direction de l'archéologie, programme H 17, p. 218.

relatifs aux châteaux de terre. Parmi ces questions, qui se posent cas par cas mais pour presque tous les sites, on trouve:

- l'origine de la fortification et la date de sa construction, le contexte historique de celle-ci,
- la nature exacte de la fortification initiale: enceinte ou motte, avec ou sans basse-cour, le nombre de ces basses-cours, ainsi que leur fonction ?
- l'emplacement et l'organisation respective des bâtiments érigés sur le site
- les accès: comment accédait-on à la fortification, comment l'entrée était-elle aménagée ?

D'autres questions sont spécifiques à chaque site:

- qui habite le château[25] ? Un prince (un roi, un prince territorial, un comte, un évêque) ou un seigneur de la moyenne aristocratie, ou encore un *milites* ou un alleutier ?
- quelles sont les causes de la construction (contexte historique): période d'affaiblissement du pouvoir central, rivalités seigneuriales, frontière, défrichement,
- quelle est l'évolution du site après sa construction,
- pourquoi le site est-il abandonné?

Pour répondre à ces questions plusieurs conditions sont impératives, nous allons tenter d'en dresser la liste.

1) Le bon état de conservation de la fortification

Ce "bon état", pour tout relatif qu'il soit, est fondamental, qu'il s'agisse d'une enceinte de terre ou d'une motte, en effet les sites de terre sont très sujets à l'érosion, aussi bien les tertres et les remparts que les fossés qui tendent peu à peu à se combler.

Trois exemples peuvent illustrer ce point. Notre-Dame-de-Gravenchon[26], en Seine-Maritime, est une enceinte à double basse-cour. La défense du château est assurée par un talus en arc de cercle haut de plus de 8 m du côté est, le plus exposé, et qui s'abaisse progressivement vers l'ouest et la rivière. Une première basse-cour enserre complètement la fortification. Une seconde fortification au nord, moins bien défendue, complète le dispositif. Les reliefs étaient

[25] A. Debord, "À propos de l'utilisation des mottes castrales", *Château Gaillard*, XI, *Études de castellologie médiévale*, Caen, 1983, pp. 91-99 et particulièrement pp. 96-98.

[26] Cf. *supra* et 1987, *Les châteaux normands de Guillaume le Conquérant à Richard Cœur de Lion*, Publication du musée de Normandie, n° 6, Caen, pp. 26-27.

bien conservés, une chapelle avait été ultérieurement édifiée dans l'enceinte, mais elle n'occupait qu'une petite proportion de la surface totale[27].

La motte d'Olivet à Grimbosq (Calvados) est située sur la partie terminale d'un éperon formé par le confluent de deux vallées profondes aux versants abrupts. Les rivières après le confluent se jettent dans l'Orne. Pour former la motte, on a creusé un fossé circulaire dans la roche schisteuse en place et une partie des terres retirées a été reportée au sommet qui s'élevait à 7 m au-dessus du sol environnant. En avant, vers le nord, une basse-cour a été aménagée à la pointe de l'éperon, à l'abri d'un rempart de terre tandis qu'un fossé était creusé en contrebas. Au sud de la motte, une deuxième basse-cour s'étendait, elle occupait tout l'espace de l'éperon qui est beaucoup plus large à cet endroit. Elle était entièrement ceinturée d'un rempart de terre précédé, vers l'extérieur, d'un fossé. Plus au sud, une autre levée de terre en arc de cercle, également précédée d'un fossé, barrait l'éperon[28]. Couverte d'un taillis de petits chênes, la motte d'Olivet n'avait fait l'objet d'aucune construction récente, les reliefs étaient bien préservés favorisant l'étude.

Enfin, la "Butte du château" à Bretoncelles[29] (Orne) (Fig. 1) est située sur une ligne de crête, en position dominante par rapport à la vallée et aux cours d'eau: la Corbionne, à l'ouest, et l'un de ses affluents, au sud-est. La motte, très puissante (15 m de haut) mesure environ 45 m à sa base et 18 m au sommet, elle domine une basse-cour ovalaire entourée d'une levée de terre et d'un fossé profond. L'entrée, située à l'est est protégée par une barbacane en croissant. Ce terre-plein est lui-même entouré d'une seconde basse-cour qui l'englobe presque totalement et qui s'incline en direction du sud-est. Un rempart enserre cet espace. Bien marqué lorsqu'il se raccorde à la fortification principale, il disparaît vers le bas de la pente au sud-est. Le fossé, bien plus profond à ses extrémités s'estompe également. La basse-cour est limitée dans cette direction par un talus très pentu. Il s'agit ā nouveau d'un site en milieu forestier, dépourvu de constructions récentes et aux reliefs encore bien marqués.

2) Un contexte historique et géographique bien étudié

Fréquemment, l'installation de la fortification découle de la dynamique du peuplement et de la présence de voies de communication. L'étude conduite par

---

27 J.-M. Cahagne (dir.), *Notre-Dame de Gravenchon. Deux mille ans d'histoire,* Ville de Notre-Dame-de-Gravenchon, et plus particulièrement, par J. Le Maho, "Le temps des seigneurs"dans "De l'Antiquité à la fin du Moyen Âge", 2000, pp. 32-69.

28 Cf. Decaëns, *op. cit.,* 1981, p. 169.

29 J. Decaëns, "Bretoncelles (Orne), La butte du Château, Chronique des fouilles médiévales en France", *Archéologie Médiévale,* 23, 1993, pp. 414; "Bretoncelles (Orne), La butte du Château, Chronique des fouilles médiévales en France", *Archéologie Médiévale,* 26, 1996, pp. 275-277; "Bretoncelles (Orne), La butte du Château, Chronique des fouilles médiévales en France", *Archéologie Médiévale,* 27, Caen, 1997, p. 226; "Bretoncelles (Orne), La butte du Château, Chronique des fouilles médiévales en France", *Archéologie Médiévale,* 28, Caen, 1998, p. 262; A.-M. Flambard Héricher, "Bretoncelles, la 'Butte du château'", *Bilan scientifique 1999,* Direction Régionale des Affaires Culturelles de Basse-Normandie, Service Régional de l'Archéologie, 1999, pp. 76-78; A.-M. Flambard Héricher, Ph. Bernouis et J. Decaëns, *op. cit.,* 2000.

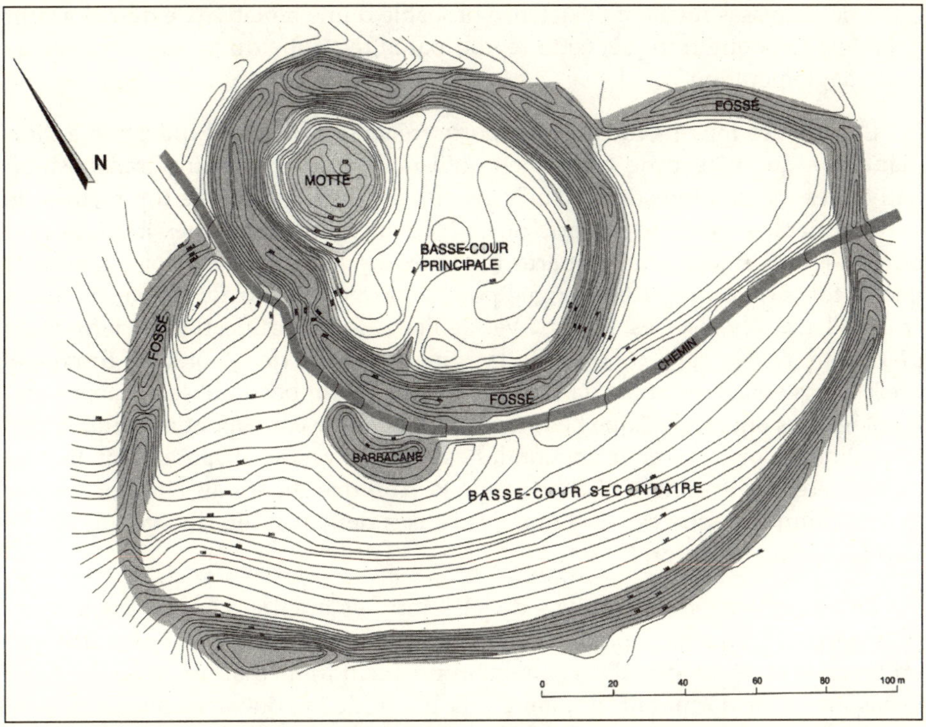

Fig. 1. Bretoncelles plan général de la "Butte du château" (relevé et dessin Ph. Bernouis et A.-M. Flambard Héricher).

E. Zadora Rio autour de la fortification du Plessis-Grimoult[30] est dans ce domaine exemplaire. Après avoir cartographié les découvertes archéologiques[31], les toponymes gaulois, les toponymes gallo-romains et les toponymes germaniques, elle a relevé le découpage des paroisses et la répartition des dédicaces paroissiales (à Saint-Sauveur et Sainte-Croix, Saint-Martin, Saint-Pierre et à la Vierge)[32], et enfin la répartition des fortifications: enceinte, motte, château de pierre ainsi que les ouvrages détruits ou non localisés[33]. Cette étude a révélé, à l'intérieur de l'honneur du Plessis-Grimoult, deux parties distinctes: le sud-est forme une région qui porte des traces de la présence humaine depuis le néolithique et qui a connu à l'époque romaine une colonisation importante, puis un peuplement franc dont la permanence est démontrée par l'archéologie et la toponymie, et confirmée par les vocables paroissiaux. À l'inverse la partie occidentale de l'honneur ne présente aucun indice archéologique ou topographique de colonisation avant le second millénaire de notre ère: "... bien que les dédi-

[30] E. Zadora Rio, *op. cit.*, 1973-1974, pp. 113 à 122.

[31] *Ibid.*, p. 115, fig. 2, Répartition des trouvailles archéologiques. Sur cette carte figurent les découvertes d'objets, de mégalithes ou tumulus, de bâtiments, de camps, de monastères, de sarcophages, ainsi que les voies romaines.

[32] *Ibid.*, p. 119, fig. 6, Répartition des dédicaces paroissiales.

[33] *Ibid.*, p. 120, fig. 7, Répartition des fortifications.

caces de paroisses révèlent l'existence probable d'une tentative de défrichement avortée à l'époque franque, cette région paraît, à l'aube du XIe siècle vierge de toute agglomération"[34].

L'étude des massifs forestiers apporte fréquemment une explication à l'implantation du château de terre, bien qu'il faille se garder d'une transposition hâtive des massifs forestiers actuels en massifs médiévaux. Les toponymes de défrichements comme les essarts ou la Neuville, des toponymes liés à la présence d'arbres aujourd'hui disparus (Le Quesnay, le hameau du bois.) montrent que la fortification a pu être érigée pour mettre en valeur de nouvelles terres et installer des hôtes; c'est le cas à Vatteville-la-Rue[35], fortification de terre et de pierre qui s'élève sur les bords de la Seine en lisière de la forêt de Brotonne. C'est le cas également pour la motte d'Olivet à Grimbosq où des analyses palynologiques ont montré que l'édification de la motte correspondait à une transformation du paysage environnant, les essences silvestres disparaissant au profit des céréales; il semble d'ailleurs que la pauvreté du sol ait entraîné l'échec de ces cultures et que ce soit l'une des causes de l'abandon du site qui est retourné, ensuite, à la forêt.

La multiplication des fouilles de sites fortifiés montre aussi de manière de plus en plus fréquente, que le château s'installe souvent sur un site artisanal ou favorise et développe dans son environnement immédiat un artisanat. C'est le cas au Plessis-Grimoult, implanté à la limite de la zone anciennement colonisée et des friches, sur une construction légère du Xe siècle comportant un four qui avait peut-être une fonction métallurgique[36]. Au Thuit (commune de Boulon, Calvados) et à Bretoncelles (Orne) les scories recueillies en quantités considérables, auxquelles s'ajoute, à Bretoncelles, le nombre de fours découverts sur le site, indiquent bien l'importance de la métallurgie au sein même du château. Dans ce dernier cas, cette activité a perduré tout en se déplaçant vers les fonds de vallée qui permettent des aménagements hydrauliques. Il faut souligner qu'on est là dans le Perche, où le minerai est partout présent, notamment dans les zones forestières[37].

Enfin le réseau hydrographique enregistre souvent les traces d'aménagements liés à la présence du château: étangs et viviers sont fréquents, les moulins nécessitent des dérivations dont la trace perdure dans le paysage. La présence seigneuriale se traduit aussi par d'autres aménagements tels que les ga-

---

34 *Ibid.*, p. 241.

35 A.-M. Flambard Héricher, "Premiers résultats des fouilles du château de Vatteville-la-Rue (Seine Maritime)", *Château Gaillard, XVII, Études de castellologie européenne,* Caen, 1996, pp. 85-89; *Id.*, "La construction dans la Basse vallée de la Seine, l'exemple du château de Vatteville-la-Rue", *Château Gaillard, XVII, Études de castellologie européenne,* Caen, 1998, pp. 93-102; Id., "La cuisine du logis seigneurial du 'Vieux château' de Vatteville-la-Rue (Seine-Maritime)", *Autour du château médiéval,* Mémoires et documents nº 1, Société historique et Archéologique de l'Orne, 1998b, pp. 131-145; *Id.*, "Le *shell-keep* de Vatteville-la-Rue (Seine-Maritime)", *Les relations entre la Haute-Normandie et le sud de l'Angleterre, Proximus, II,* Rouen, 1998c, pp. 169-177.

36 E. Zadora Rio, *op. cit.*, 1973-1974, p. 241.

37 A.V., *La métallurgie normande, la révolution du haut-fourneau,* Cahiers de l'inventaire, Caen, 1991, notamment pp. 44-46, 53, 56, 58, 61-62, 65-67, 81, 185, 191, 195-196, 203, 214, 228.

rennes et les parcs à gibiers qui couvrent parfois plusieurs centaines d'hectares: Notre-Dame-de-Gravenchon, Vatteville-la-Rue, le château de Caen étaient concernés par de tels aménagements.

Au repérage des éléments encore en place (église paroissiale, noyau d'habitat, abbaye, prieuré) doit s'ajouter la recherche documentaire dans les textes qui peut dans certains cas être fructueuse (Plessis-Grimoult, Vatteville-la-Rue), dans d'autres cas médiocre (Grimbosq), dans d'autres cas encore, très fréquents, totalement stérile (Château Ganne à La Pommeraye, Bretoncelles).

Le bon état de conservation d'une seule partie de la fortification peut parfois suffire à justifier une fouille. À Rivray par exemple, où des mentions du site apparaissent dans les archives, où la fortification est incomplète, où la basse-cour ou les basses-cours ont disparu, un bâtiment d'époque romane installé sur le fossé subsiste[38]; des critères topographiques architecturaux et stratigraphiques permettent de placer sa construction au XIIe siècle tandis que la fortification de terre remonte au XIe siècle. L'étude intrinsèque des vestiges de la motte (avec les restes de tour maçonnée qui la couronnent) et du bâtiment roman s'est révélée riche d'enseignement.

3ÈME TEMPS: LA FOUILLE

1) Les recherches préliminaires

Avant de procéder à la fouille d'un site, il est nécessaire, si cela n'a pas déjà été fait, de procéder au relevé détaillé de la topographie du terrain et de confirmer l'intérêt du site en procédant à des sondages. L'implantation de ces derniers permet de vérifier l'état de conservation des vestiges enfouis. Certains emplacements stratégiques doivent être tout particulièrement visés, parmi eux se trouve le sommet de la motte si des vestiges y subsistent malgré l'érosion, ou la surface enclose par l'enceinte. Grimbosq est un contre exemple, le sommet de la motte qui est très exigu a été entièrement bouleversé par un nid de mitrailleuse installé au cours de la seconde guerre mondiale. Le fouiller ne présentait donc aucun intérêt.

L'entrée, quand on en soupçonne l'emplacement, mérite d'être étudiée, ainsi, à Bretoncelles: une chaussée empierrée à été mise en évidence. Des murs latéraux et des claveaux découverts sur le sol montrent qu'une tour-porche surmontée d'un arc contrôlait l'accès à la fortification. L'entrée de l'enceinte du Plessis-Grimoult était défendue également par une tour porche maçonnée. Tandis que des tours de bois surmontaient l'entrée de Notre-Dame de Gravenchon.

Le relevé topographique réalisé permet aussi de mieux repérer des reliefs ou micro-reliefs qui peuvent être révélateurs. Ainsi, à Bretoncelles un monticule situé au centre de la basse-cour s'est révélé être un four à pain dont la sole et

---

38 J. Decaëns, *op. cit.*, 1992, p. 31.

l'âtre sont encore bien conservés tandis que le manteau s'est effondré sur le sol quand le linteau de bois qui le soutenait à cédé.

Un sondage préliminaire permet également d'évaluer la puissance de la stratigraphie et sa complexité, et de mettre en évidence la présence d'un éventuel état antérieur. Au Plessis-Grimoult, un four correspondant à une occupation primitive était recouvert par l'enceinte de terre, à Mirville, c'est un bâtiment de bois qui avait été recouvert par la motte. À Notre-Dame de Gravenchon, une chapelle de pierre s'est superposée aux constructions de bois. La nécessité de conduire des recherches sur des sites peu remaniés apparaît bien ici. Les vestiges de l'occupation primitive étant ténus, on comprend pourquoi les fouilles des grands châteaux de pierre sont si peu révélatrices quant aux premiers aménagements du site.

En outre certains éléments, qui ne peuvent faire l'objet d'une fouille en grande surface, doivent être mis en évidence par de simples tranchées exploratoires. Il est ainsi judicieux de connaître le mode de construction du rempart, mais il est impossible de le fouiller totalement. Une coupe est nécessaire pour connaître les matériaux qui le constituent: terre, terre et bois, terre et pierre et pour déceler les éventuels rehaussements ou les reprises. En revanche, des sondages au sommet de ce même rempart peuvent permettre de repérer les trous de poteaux laissés par une palissade ou un chemin de ronde, toutefois l'effet de l'érosion rend cette recherche souvent aléatoire.

La manière d'aborder l'étude des fossés est un peu la même. Dans ce cas encore, une coupe permet d'en connaître le profil et de repérer d'éventuels réaménagements. Les fonds de fossés sont aussi souvent des dépotoirs privilégiés qui permettent de connaître la vie matérielle sur le site et de donner des repères chronologiques. Il est notamment possible d'y mettre en évidence des recreusements et des reprises qui témoignent tantôt d'un entretien courant, tantôt de profondes réfections.

L'accès à la motte à partir de la basse-cour est un point qu'il convient d'étudier en complément des recherches sur l'entrée et auquel des sondages peuvent répondre. La tapisserie de Bayeux présente certains modes d'accès comme des passerelles enjambant le fossé que l'archéologie a pu confirmer ainsi, à Grimbosq (Fig. 2) des trous de poteaux repérés sur le flanc de la motte ont permis d'imaginer une passerelle d'accès qui depuis un bâtiment situé dans la basse-cour résidentielle permettait de gagner le sommet.

2) La fouille en aire ouverte

Même si les sondages évoqués plus haut répondent à un certain nombre de questions, seule la fouille exhaustive permet de connaître l'organisation d'un site. Cette fouille en aire ouverte peut être appliquée au sommet de la motte s'il est suffisamment bien préservé, mais elle est particulièrement fructueuse quand elle est pratiquée sur la basse-cour qui s'avère fréquemment beaucoup plus riche d'enseignements que la motte elle-même.

Fig. 2. Reconstitution du site de Grimbosq (Dessin Y. Le Tort, Service Départemental d'Archéologie du Calvados).

La fouille doit viser à mettre en évidence les principaux éléments fonctionnels du château: la grande salle *(aula)* et les appartements privés *(camera);* les éléments de défense: tours, donjon, palissade, chemin de ronde, pont-levis, système fossoyé; la chapelle; les éléments de la vie domestique: cuisine, caves, celliers, fours, puits et citernes, éléments de stockage divers; les écuries et la forge; la présence d'animaux élevés ou domestiqués. La présence de tous ces éléments n'est pas obligatoire, certains, tels la chapelle, pouvant être absents ou mobiles (il existait des chapelles portatives). D'autres fonctions peuvent se placer à l'étage ou ailleurs (sur la motte ou dans une seconde basse-cour) et n'avoir laissé de ce fait, aucune trace dans la zone étudiée. Un certain nombre de fouilles conduites en Normandie sont remarquables par les résultats qu'elles ont apportés dans l'un ou l'autre de ces domaines.

La fouille de Grimbosq a révélé l'organisation d'un site fortifié (cf. Fig. 2). La motte en position centrale, d'assez petite taille flanquée d'une basse-cour résidentielle à la pointe de l'éperon et d'une basse-cour domestique à l'opposé. L'*aula,* la cuisine,.la chapelle ont été mis en évidence ainsi qu'un bâtiment permettant l'accès à la motte, la nature de l'appareil a été déterminée: du pan-de-bois sur solin de schiste tandis que les bâtiments légers de la seconde basse-cour étaient bâtis en bois.

La fouille de Bretoncelles (Fig. 3) qui n'est pas achevée n'a pas encore concerné l'ensemble de la basse-cour mais environ la moitié. Elle a permis de mettre en évidence, au pied de la motte, un petit bâtiment de silex qui comportait sans doute un étage et possédait une cheminée à contrecœur semi-circulaire. Dans un second temps un bâtiment est venu s'appuyer contre la cheminée, accroissant l'espace résidentiel qui se situait à l'étage (Fig. 4). Un vaste bâtiment de bois sur solin de calcaire, à claire-voie au nord, lui faisait face, il abritait un four

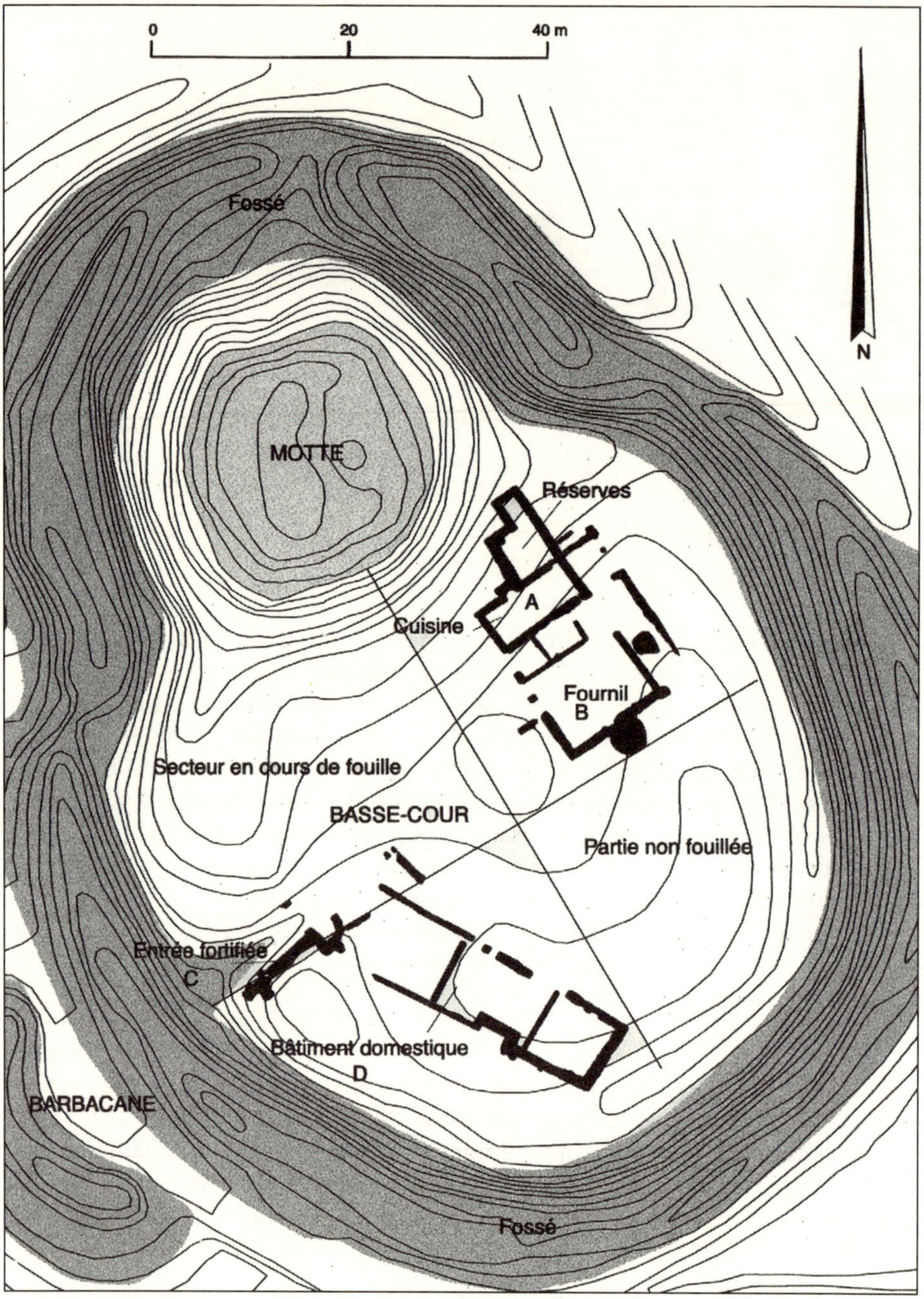

Fig. 3. Les bâtiments découverts dans la basse-cour de la "Butte du Château" à Bretoncelles (Dessin Ph. Bernouis, A.-M. Flambard Héricher, B. Lepeuple).

à pain. À ses côtés se trouvait un second four dont la fonction reste mystérieuse mais dont on peut souligner la proximité avec le four à pain. Dans le secteur opposé s'allongeait un édifice en pan-de-bois sur solin de silex de 26 m de long et 7 m de large, jouxtant vraisemblablement une tour–porche. La fouille a ré-

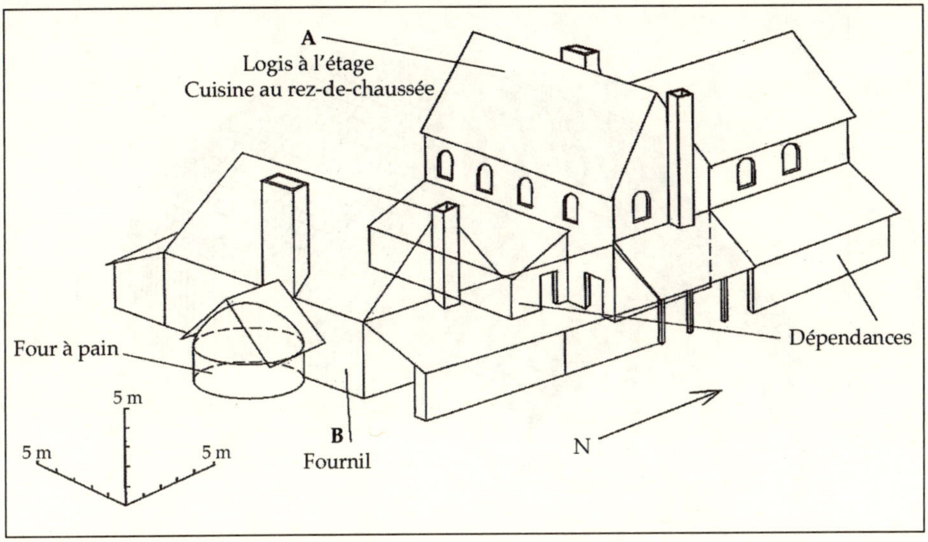

Fig. 4. Bâtiments résidentiels et domestiques fortement imbriqués dans la basse-cour de la fortification de Bretoncelles (Dessin A.-M. Flambard Héricher).

vélé la chronologie de ce bâtiment qui a succédé à un bâtiment sur poteaux, remplacé d'abord par un bâtiment sur solin de dimensions réduites qui abritait un four puis, dans un second temps ce bâtiment fut allongé jusqu'à atteindre 26 m, tandis que le four était détruit et reconstruit sur le même emplacement. La métallurgie est présente partout sur le site sans que l'on puisse encore déterminer avec précision comment la production était organisée. L'aménagement de la basse-cour, les différents bâtiments et leur évolution, l'importance de l'artisanat ont bien été mis en évidence lors de la fouille qui devrait apporter encore de nombreux renseignements sur la fortification et son évolution.

La fouille exhaustive de la motte de Mirville, qui a été conduite jusqu'au substrat par J. Le Maho à montré comment il est possible de révéler les traces d'une habitation antérieure, ici il s'agissait d'une habitation de bois. Elle a permis la reconstitution d'une maison du XIe siècle (Fig. 5) très semblable aux maisons visibles sur la tapisserie de Bayeux.

Enfin les découvertes effectuées sur les sites fortifiés ont également livré un matériel très abondant qui a permis de dresser le tableau de la vie quotidienne, de l'armement, de l'alimentation, de l'équipement en armes et du harnachement, pour ne citer que ces quelques exemples, ce fut le cas à Vatteville-la-Rue, notamment.

CONCLUSION

Malheureusement, la fouille des fortifications de terre est aujourd'hui devenue très rare. Les travaux réalisés sur les châteaux concernent davantage les

Fig. 5. Reconstitution de la maison de Mirville (d'après Le Maho J., 1984, op. cit.).

bâtiments sur lesquels des restaurations doivent être entreprises, et il s'agit souvent de sondages limités, qui ne nous livrent que des éléments de connaissance ponctuels. Quelques grands sites ont fait, récemment, l'objet de fouilles très étendues: il s'agit du château d'Angers et de celui de Mayenne qui s'est révélé être d'origine carolingienne. Mais ce sont des fortifications de pierre, imposantes, et non de petites fortifications de terre, beaucoup plus ingrates à fouiller, mais dont l'apport global est loin d'être négligeable. Si l'origine de ces fortifications reste inconnue, on découvre parfois, comme cela était apparu avec l'étude de la motte de Doué-la-Fontaine, que les sites ont connu une occupation avant de devenir une motte. En Normandie, c'est le cas au Plessis-Grimoult et à Mirville. Tous les problèmes posés par ces fortifications sont loin d'être résolus. Leur aménagement interne reste souvent mal connu. Il est par conséquent à souhaiter que de recherches reprennent sur ce thème qui est loin d'être épuisé, mais qui connaît actuellement un recul par rapport à l'étude des fortifications de pierre.

SOME IDEAS ON SOCIAL STRUCTURE AND SYSTEM OF THE NORTHERNMOST VIKINGS

Reidar Bertelsen
University of Tromsø

In the southern 2/3 of Scandinavia, the Viking Period (a.D. 750-1050) marks the transition between the Iron Age and the Medieval period. This was an important period when it came to the formation of states and the establishment of Christianity marked the division between the Viking and the Medieval periods.

The northern frontier of the Viking world has its northernmost corner on the coast of North Norway. It has also been described as the frontier of farming (Sjøvold, 1974, pp. 334-357). The key factor has been seen as the climatic border for cereals (ca 69° 30′ N). The division between Hálogaland and Finnmork as mentioned in several sagas, coincides largely with this frontier. The people of Hálogaland were the northernmost of the Norse Vikings and the people of Finnmork, the Sami, were outside (Fig. 1).

The famous Ottar (Othere) who visited the court in Wessex shortly before a.D. 900 and told that he was the northernmost of permanently settled men. He has therefore entered the archaeological and historical literature as the Viking frontier in person.

Although new information has come to light and new analyses have been made during the years after Sjøvold's book, nobody has really questioned his model of the Late Iron Age society, a basically agricultural society that used the wildlife resources of the country mostly through exchange relations with their neighbours, the Sami.

Roger Jørgensen (1984) added archaeological and osteological evidence from two sites on the island of Andøy (Bleik and Toften) indicating that at least deep sea fish and sea mammals had been important sources of energy. In a summary of new research, Olav Sverre Johansen stated that the economy of the Iron Age farms must have been mixed and varied. He also wrote that the farm was the core of the Norse Iron Age society and that the high status farms were located were the conditions for cattle and cereals were optimal (1990). These conclusions builds on work by among others: Berglund, Bertelsen, Holand, Holm-

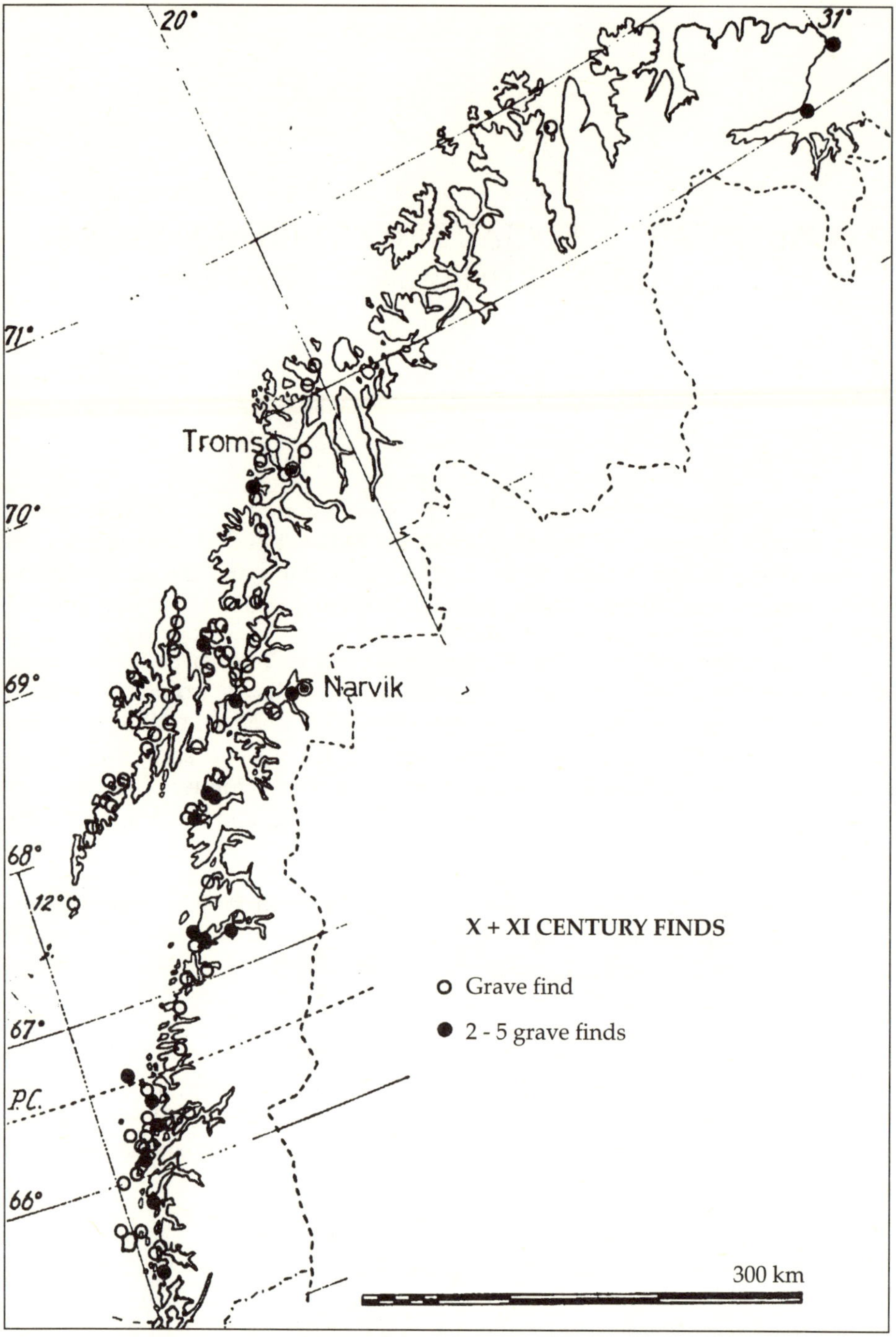

Fig. 1. A map of Late Viking Period Finds (Sjøvold, 1974, p. 343). The distribution of finds indicates the extents of Hálogaland. Finnmork is to the East and to the North.

Olsen, Johansen, Jørgensen, Moltu, Schanche, Stamsø Munch, Storli, Stom Munch and Vorren.

Audhild Schanche's work (1986) stressed one important aspect which had been observed before, but not studied systematically. The Iron Age settlement of the region that later became known as Hálogaland, was not a homogenous Norse region, it consisted of an ethnic interlace of Sami and Norse communities whereas the region to the East and North were almost exclusively Sami.

During the1990-ies, new surveys and test excavations in the Lofoten and Vesterålen islands have made it clear that this picture of economic variation and ethnic interlace are facing new challenges (Bertelsen, 1999). Norse long houses and Iron Age graves have been discovered on locations where it is hard to believe that substantial agricultural activity could have taken place. The livelihood must have been based on marine resources (fish and sea mammals). Furthermore, the lack of conformity within Norse settlements makes it difficult to identify any difference between Sami and Norse settlements when it comes to economy.

These observations challenge our conventional model of the Norse society on the threshold of the Medieval Period. Even if it has been realized that the economy of the northern farm also was based on marine resources, the terrestrial resources and the rules related to these resources have always been regarded as the key elements in the social system of the Iron Age.

Understanding the character of the spatial division between Norse and Sami is an equally demanding research challenge. How can we conceive a multi ethnic, Norse dominated Hálogaland with a diffuse border zone towards Finnmork, also being multi ethnic, but dominated by Sami groups?

These questions are far too complex to be dealt with in a short paper and the project I am referring to is only in its first stage. I shall only address the question of the social system of Hálogaland on the edge between the prehistoric and the historic era.

THE FARM

The northern Norwegian farm from the 17th to the 20th centuries have been studied carefully by historians with contributions from archaeologists and ethnologists (see Bratrein, 1989, for a general presentation). It has been named the "combination farm" and its main features are:

- A single holding settlement close to the shoreline.
- A relatively small property.
- A herd consisting of cattle, sheep, goats and one horse.
- Small patchy fields (in early times for barley, later for potatoes).

- Market oriented fisheries (mainly winter cod, but also saithe, halibut, herring etc.).
- Extensive hunting of marine and terrestrial mammals and birds.

The organization of space were in accordance with the above features:

- A yard with a domestic building and a cowshed.
- Fenced home fields.
- Outlying areas, generally used for grazing in cooperation with neighbours.
- A boathouse and a landing place for open boats (square sail).
- The majority of the boats went to the Lofoten and Vesterålen islands for winter fisheries.
- In the fishing villages, the crew stayed in a cottage which they rented or in rare cases owned.

The economic activities and the space were subject to a rather well defined gender related division were the farmer was female and the fisherman was male. During short periods of the year the fishermen took part in the harvest. Likewise, the women supplied provisions and clothes for the fishing expeditions. This economic and social system was common amongst the Norse as well as the Coastal Sami ethnic groups. The only difference may have been that the gender division seemed more clearly emphasised among the Norse than among the Sami.

Even if changes have been identified in this system during the period through which it has been studied, it seems to have been fairly stable and it is generally thought to be valid for the entire Medieval and Post Medieval era. It has not been believed that this system goes further back than to the beginning of the market oriented fisheries, probably in the 11th century. Related to this assumption it has also been assumed that fisheries played a lesser role as an economic and social resource in the Iron Age than in the Medieval period. The corresponding picture of the Iron Age has been that agriculture was the dominant social and economic resource of the social system even if evidence of a broad spectrum economy has been observed. Most authors have suggested that this variation could be interpreted within the frames of a redistributive system with a number of chieftains as the core figures, spatially organized in a chain along the coast (described in detail by Berglund, 1995 and Hansen, 2000, pp. 58-66). A typical Iron Age chieftain's site was a large farm on a place where the conditions for agriculture were optimal and at the same time a strategic crossing of communication lines.

The whole model of the Iron Age social system is based on at least three assumptions:

- That agriculture has a built-in capacity to take over as a dominant social and economical resource in any pre-industrial society.
- That a redistribution system is the most likely pre-state social system and that power is rooted in the control of economic resources.
- That pre-modern social systems tend to be homogenous or conform.

It is interesting to observe that these assumptions are contrary to main trends in recent sociological thinking. Anthony Giddens, in his *Theory of Structuration,* argues for a much more complex understanding of how social systems are constructed and interact (1981). At this stage of the work, it is not possible to give a detailed discussion of the subject in the light of new data and new alternative theoretical models. Some possibilities shall however be pointed out referring to Giddens' theory.

First, there is no given direction of social change. Second, the individual actors make choices that only partly can be presupposed as a consequence of rules. Given the context, the freedom of choice for a *knowledgeable actor* may differ largely. And not the least, power is established and reproduced on basis of a number of different resources, *allocative and authoritative.*

This means that a web of social systems are conceivable at the same time within the same region. Life at sea may have one system where important resources are such as a safe and good landing place, a good boat, knowledge and skills that are necessary for getting a plentiful catch and a safe journey in rough waters.

Life on land may have another system where property, stored produced goods, workforce and social relations with peers are more important. Given the existence of spatially related gender divisions as well as ethnic differences in space and time, this allows for exiting alternatives for *social and system integration* other than redistribution. Integration with outside systems may have made possible a hierarchic structure with large farms as nodes.

These ideas opens up a line of thinking that may lead to an explanation of the general observation that the spatial distribution of settlements as well as the character of settlements were more diverse in the Iron Age than in the Medieval period.

BIBLIOGRAPHY

BERGLUND, I.B. (1995): *Tjøtta-riket. En arkeologisk undersøkelse av maktforhold og sentrumsdannelser på helgelandskysten fra Kr.f til 1700 e.Kr.,* Dr. Thesis, University of Trondheim.

BERTELSEN, R. (1999): "Settlement on the divide between land and ocean. From Iron Age to Medieval Period along the coast of Northern Norway", in Fabech and Ringtved (eds.), *Settlement and Landscape,* Jutland Archaeological Society, Århus.

BRATREIN, H.D. (1989): *Karlsøy og Helgøy Bygdebok,* Vol. I, Fra steinalder til år 1700, Hansnes.

GIDDENS, A. (1981): *Contemporary Critique of Historical Materialism,* 2nd edition, 1995, McMillan, London.

HANSEN, L.I. (2000): *Astafjord bygdebok,* Vol. 1, Fra eldre jernalder til ca 1570, Lavangen.

JOHANSEN, O.S. (1990): *Synspunkter på jernalderens jordbrukssamfunn i Nord-Norge,* University of Tromsø, Social Science series B, nº 20.

JØRGENSEN, R. (1984): *Bleik. En økonomisk/økologisk studie av grunnlaget for jernaldergården på Andøya i Nordland,* Thesis, University of Tromsø.

SCHANCHE, A. (1986): *Nordnorsk jernalderarkeologi. Et sosialgeografisk perspektiv,* Thesis, University of Tromsø.

SJØVOLD, T. (1974): *The Iron Age of Arctic Norway, Vol. II,* Norwegian University Press, Tromsø, Oslo, Bergen.

POZNAŃ-*SEDES REGNIPRINCIPALES* AT THE BEGINNING OF THE POLISH PIAST STATE

HANNA KÓČKA-KRENZ
Adam Mickiewicz University, Poznań, Poland

The beginning of Poznań, currently one of the major Polish cities, goes back to the early Middle Ages, since at the end of the 9th century the first inhabitants started to settle in Ostrów Tumski. The archeologists' interest in Ostrów Tumski in Poznań can be traced back to the beginning of the 20th century, although, at first, it was limited to the "surface research" and actions accompanying earthworks. The planned excavations were started in 1938 by the team of archeologists from the contemporary Institute of Prehistory at Poznań University led by Prof. Józef Kostrzewski. At that time already excavations were oriented to find the Poznań Early Medieval town, one of the centers of early Piast monarchy[1]. The works were stopped by the outbreak of the World War II and they were resumed in 1946 (basically, they have been in progress since the early 60's). The later research was of the rescue character, although it also contributed to the discovery of important data concerning both the defensive character of the stronghold and its chronology. In 1999, the Institute of Prehistory at Poznań University took to the planned research in Ostrów Tumski with the purpose of excavating the relics of the pre-Romanesque sacral-palace complex, existence of which was often suggested in the literature devoted to the abovementioned subject[2]. Current exploration, though it affected only a small part of the site occupied by the early Piast stronghold, thanks to its being situated in different spots of Ostrów Tumski allowed for the reconstruction of the consecutive phases of its settlement and development[3]. In accordance with the results

1 *Poznań we wczesnym średniowieczu,* ed. W. Hensel, Warszawa-Wrocław, 1, 1959, pp. 7-9.

2 Z. Pianowski, *Sedes regni principales. Wawel i inne rezydencje piastowskie do połowy XIII wieku na tle europejskim,* Kraków, 1997, p. 52; M. Kara, "Początki i rozwój wczesnośredniowiecznego ośrodka grodowego na Ostrowie Tumskim w Poznaniu", *Civitates principales. Wybrane ośrodki władzy w Polsce wczesnośredniowiecznej,* Gniezno, 1998, p. 28.

3 W. Hensel, Z. Hilczer-Kurnatowska, *Studia i materiały do osadnictwa Wielkopolski wczesnohistorycznej,* Wroclaw, 1980, 5, pp. 147-149; M. Kara, "Początki rozwój wczesnośredniowiecznego ośrodka grodowego na Ostrowie Tumskim w Poznaniu", *Civitates principales. Wybrane ośrodki władzy w Polsce wczesnośredniowiecznej,* Gniezno, 1998, pp. 26-29.

of the newest research they constitute the basis to sum up the current knowledge concerning the Poznań Early Medieval town:

In the course of Middle Ages Ostrów Tumski in Poznań was one of the sandy and dump islands formed by the Warta River (Fig. 1). The site was in a very advantageous point since the presence of abundant water routes and fords that set forth the long-ranging communicational routes that used to link Great Poland region with the neighboring areas. It is at this point where the roads from south to north, from the Czech territories to the opulent seaside centers crossed the land routes leading to the center of Great Poland. It enabled the inhabitants of this place to contact their vicinity and to exchange goods and ideas. What is more, during the period of the nation formation it enabled the sovereigns to subjugate the unconquered territories and to rule the whole domain. The good localization of Ostrów Tumski is further supported by the research concerning the settlement in this region. These studies proved the gradual increase of the number of inhabitants on both banks of the Warta and its estuaries since the 8th century and a considerable intensification of that phenomenon from the beginning of the 10th century.

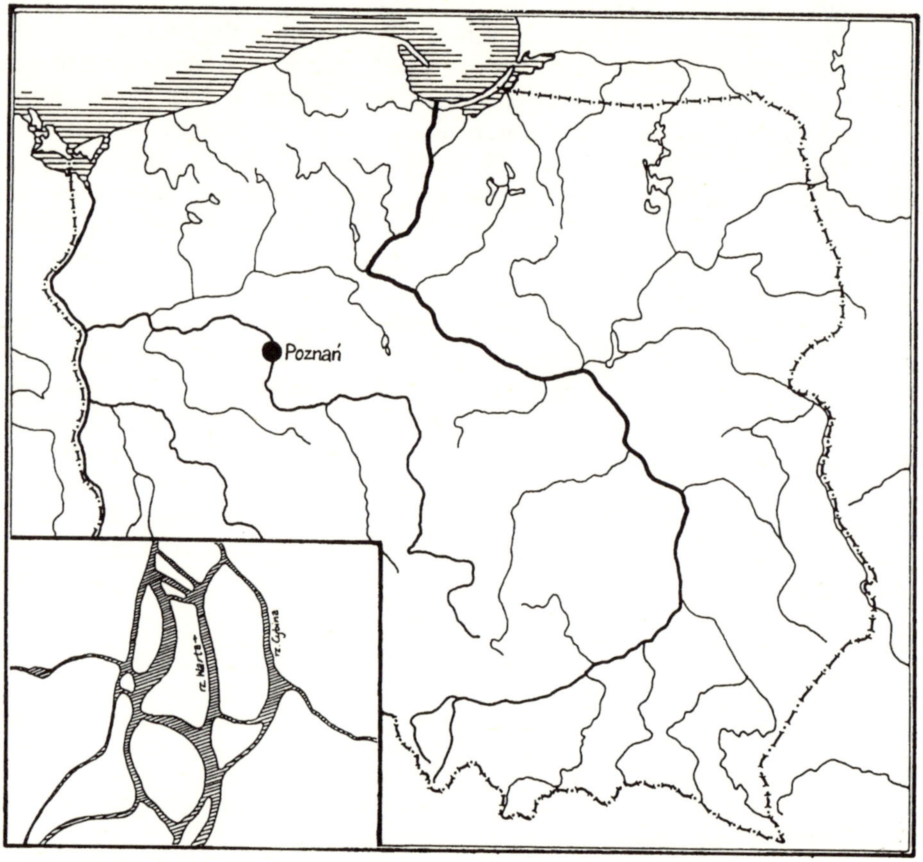

Fig. 1. Ostrów Tumski in Poznań - topographical situation.

The island situated in the fork of the Warta and the Cybina was slightly above the water surface[4] and it was divided into two parts by a swampy ditch (still visible until not long ago). Both parts had its small peaks that were settled in the first place. At the present state of research it is not yet possible to state equivocally whether this settlement happened before building here defense fortifications. The research conducted in 1999 next to St. Mary's Church seems to suggest that possibility, since the oldest settlement layers contained the fragments of pottery, which may be dated back to the beginning of the 10th century (it is further supported by the first dendrochronological analysis-year 890).

The choice of the ground to build a stronghold there is to be regarded as a very purposeful and thoroughly thought over. The analysis of the excavated parts of the fortification in both parts of this island, in accordance with the chronology, makes one think that the first stronghold was erected as a complex consisting of two main parts divided by a ditch. The first one occupied the sandy hillock north of this ditch, the second one –a similar one, south of the previously mentioned hillock– on the so-called Zagórze. One cannot be thoroughly sure as to the primal shape of the north site, of the stronghold complex. Two possibilities have to be taken into consideration –it could have been a minor, one-part construction situated on the ground currently occupied by the cathedral. It could also have been a part of a bigger, two-part foundation in the shape of a separate small stronghold (called the duke's one) surrounded by an oval ditch. It might have been placed between the building of Psaltery, St. Mary's Church and the eastern part surrounded by a horseshoe-like embankment connected to it. The author would like to opt for the second possibility bearing in mind that the analogous construction solutions were applied in the oldest part of the embankment in both parts. Furthermore, the geo-physical measurements of the shape of this island's part, supported by current excavations seem to endorse the possibility the author opts for. These excavations showed that we are dealing here with two little hillocks –one in the site of today's cathedral and the second one next to St. Mary's Church. Such the terrain shape was earlier pinpointed by W. Hensel[5] (followed by J. Żak[6]) on the basis of the research of the structure of the cultural layers near St. Mary's Church and on the Cathedral Square. One can suppose that from the very beginning all three hillocks in Ostrów Tumski were encircled by wooden-earth embankments with their base width measuring approximately 10 meters –two northern embankments: oval and horseshoe-like ones and, finally, a southern one: again a horseshoe-like embankment reaching the swampy ditch. The interior of the stronghold was packed full of wooden huts (framework construction). The remnants of these constructions, the city bath, and different household buildings (among them fireplaces and corn containers) were excavated on the Cathedral Square, close to St. Mary's

---

4 A. Kaniecki, *Poznań Dzieje miasta wodą pisane,* Poznań, 1993.

5 W. Hensel, "Na śladach Mieszkowej stolicy", *Przegląd Zachodni,* 3, pp. 123-125.

6 J. Żak, "Badania w ogrodzie przy ul. Ostrów Tumski 10 w 1946 r", *Poznań we wczesnym średniowieczu,* ed. W. Hensel, Warszawa-Wrocław, 1959, 1, pp. 115-116.

Church and in Zagórze. Tools and items destined for a variety of usage found in cultural layers are the premise for the claim that Poznań stronghold was inhabited by a group of wealthy people remaining in close connection with the ruler. On his behalf they occupied different military and administrative functions; they would also control the trade routes. The analysis of the archeological sources allows for the claim that the construction date of the first defensive embankment can be traced back to the second quarter of the 10th century. Accordingly, one can assume that the creation of the strong political center in Poznań was brought about by Mieszko's I predecessor. He is also responsible for some other main strongholds in Great Poland region, mostly Gniezno.

Shortly after the first half of the 10th century, Poznań stronghold underwent major rebuilding, especially in the two-part northern site, which dimension can be estimated as approximately 80 × 100 meters and 130 × 100 meters (Fig. 2). Older defensive fortification was partly dismantled and rebuilt, and the lower fragment of the eastern part neighboring the cathedral was used to stabilize the dumpy ground. On the verge of the 10th and 11th centuries the embankments were thoroughly expanded, their base was extended (about 20 meters) and made higher (approximately 10 meters). Furthermore, its scaffolding construction was reinforced by hooks and a broad external plinth in the lower part which made it the most powerful stronghold of those times. After the first half of the 10th century its interior was changed. The eastern part was devoted to the sacral purposes and it was manifested by the erection of a quadrangular stony building containing a big baptismal font and afterwards –a pre-Romanesque cathedral. Its shape was of the three-nave basilica with a square presbyter with apse, flanked with two annexes, closed with a western edifice surmounted with a tower. It can be assumed that the remaining development of this stronghold, just like its southern site, was still wooden, though it has been only superficially researched (in the scope of the site situated in the front of the cathedral). In the western part, the so-called "duke's", a stony, palace-sacral complex was built, whose remnants have been partially excavated recently.

The archeological premise for the search of the duke's **palatium** neighboring St. Mary's Church was brought about by the research results coming from the garden in 10 Ostrów Tumski Street (dated from 1946). The ditches running parallel to the northern wall of the church were noticed. The lowest of the noticed cultural layers contained the remnants of some wooden constructions occurring at the depth of 3.2 from the level of ground of those days. Their function was hypothetically established as the remnants of the floor (?) from the duke's buildings belonging supposedly to the *palatium* complex. It was probably erected by Władyslaw Herman in the period after the first part of the 11th century. In the middle part of this two-meter deep excavation a string of big boulders bound by clay was noticed. It was running parallel to the northern wall of the church. It mayhap constituted a remnant of the foundations whose upper part was pulled down. Because of the necessity to stop excavation it was impossible to reach the layer of its basis. Parts of newer brick walls occurring

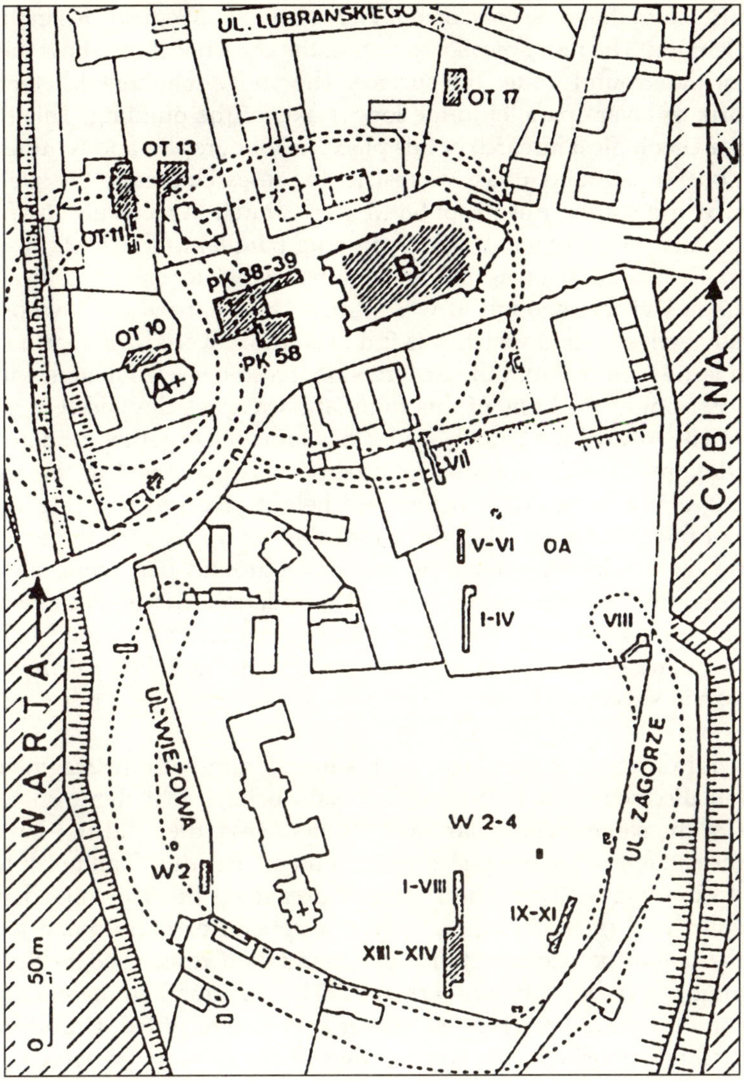

Fig. 2. The reconstruction of the reinforcing embankments of the Poznań stronghold.

above it were placed on a layer of stoned wall bound with clay. This fact led J. Żak and E. Dąbrowski to claim that these walls were erected on older foundations which previously constituted the northern part of the enclosure of the **palatium** yard (occupying the site ranging from the building of Psalter to the eastern part of St Mary's Church).

Before proceeding to further excavation the geo-physical measurements of the interior of this church and its closest neighborhood were carried out. Thanks to them a part the outline of a set of circular structures situated under the altar was detected. That may be the hint suggesting that under this part of church its older rotunda-shaped form occurs. The earlier research conducted by historians of art[7] led to the same conclusion. They observed irregularities in the gothic church planning. The radar measurements of the church vicinity show the heterogeneity of the ground under the surface. The above mentioned heterogeneity is in a form of layers parallel to the longer axis of the building. This (plus the results of archeological research of this place, its topography, and writing sources information[8]) constituted a basis to restrict the research area to the site close to the western and southern walls of St. Mary's Church. As a result, the fragment of a foundation made of small stones running parallel to the western wall was excavated. Even though it was mostly demolished by later construction activities, it still remains visible enough. It was situated in a narrow ditch whose edges were neatly veneered and which was full of stones, covered with earth and clay. Its width is 1.5 meters. From the eastern side it also has a 0.5 meters wide stone plinth, accordingly the basis of this foundation reaches the width of 2 meters. From that site toward the church wall it lies on cobbles getting under the temple foundations. Pre-Romanesque foundation was preserved in the above-described place at a length of 3 meters and height of 1.3 meters (Fig. 3). In the negative of the foundation, after the removal of its upper part, the remnants of white and pink mortar plaster from the above-ground part were found. Both the stratigraphic position of the revealed foundation, the way it was erected, and the archeological data allow for dating it back to the second half of the 10th century and claiming that it is the remnant of the duke's *palatium* belonging to Poznań stronghold.

The confrontation of the shape of this foundation with the fragment of the stony wall discovered in 1946 made scholars believe that they constitute the remnant of the same rectangular basis. Nonetheless, they did not have to belong to the same functioning phase, erected on an axis due from north to south, parallel to the Warta River. The fragment excavated in 1946 could have hold the northern wall of the building (either peripheral or partitioning wall –this possibility cannot be excluded) and the foundation researched in the current season might have hold the western wall. The last fragment belonging to the foundation of this wall reaching its corner was also recorded. Unfortunately, it was partially demolished; two bottom rows of stones were preserved. There is a clearly visible narrow sided negative of the foundation excavation on them; it is there where lumps of the mortar plaster were noticed. The excavation reaches the crossing fragment of the gothic building, construction of which destroyed the corner of *palatium.* The scrutiny of the stratigraphy on both sides of the gothic foundation allowed for the notice of the negative of pre-Romanesque foundation, pulled down thoroughly in this place. It constitutes the basis to reconstruct its shape (Fig. 4.). What is more, it was possible to record two layers containing white and pink mortar plaster, 10 cm wide layer of clay earth di-

---

[7] L. Przymusiński, "Architektura kościoła NPMarii w Poznaniu", *Biuletyn Historii Sztuki,* XVIII, 2, pp. 302-303.

[8] Z. Pianowski, *Sedes regni principales. Wawel i inne rezydencje piastowskie do połowy* XIII *wieku na tle europejskim,* Kraków, 1997, p. 50; J. Strzelczyk, *Mieszko Pierwszy,* Poznań, 1999; J. Strzelczyk, *Bolesław Chrobry,* Poznań, 1999.

Fig. 3. The fragment of the pre-Romanesque palatium' foundations.

vided these layers. The layer occurring beneath, in which lopped stones could be found, is probably the remnant of the constructional stratum of the *palatium.* The upper one was temporally interpreted as the determinant of the stratum of its interior.

Similar, though more vivid, stratigraphic setting was recorded south of the entrance to St. Mary's Church. A very loosely bound layer of big fragments of white and pink mortar plaster was recorded. Prints of stones, which were formerly bound by this mortar, were also discovered. The depth of its occurrence indicates that it constitutes the secondary deposit being the remnant of the pulled down upper parts of the pre-Romanesque building. It is unfortunately impossible to exclude the possibility of the fact that the layer in question witnessed different construction activities in the pre-Gothic period conducted in the church interior (bearing in mind its close attachment to the foundations of the Gothic

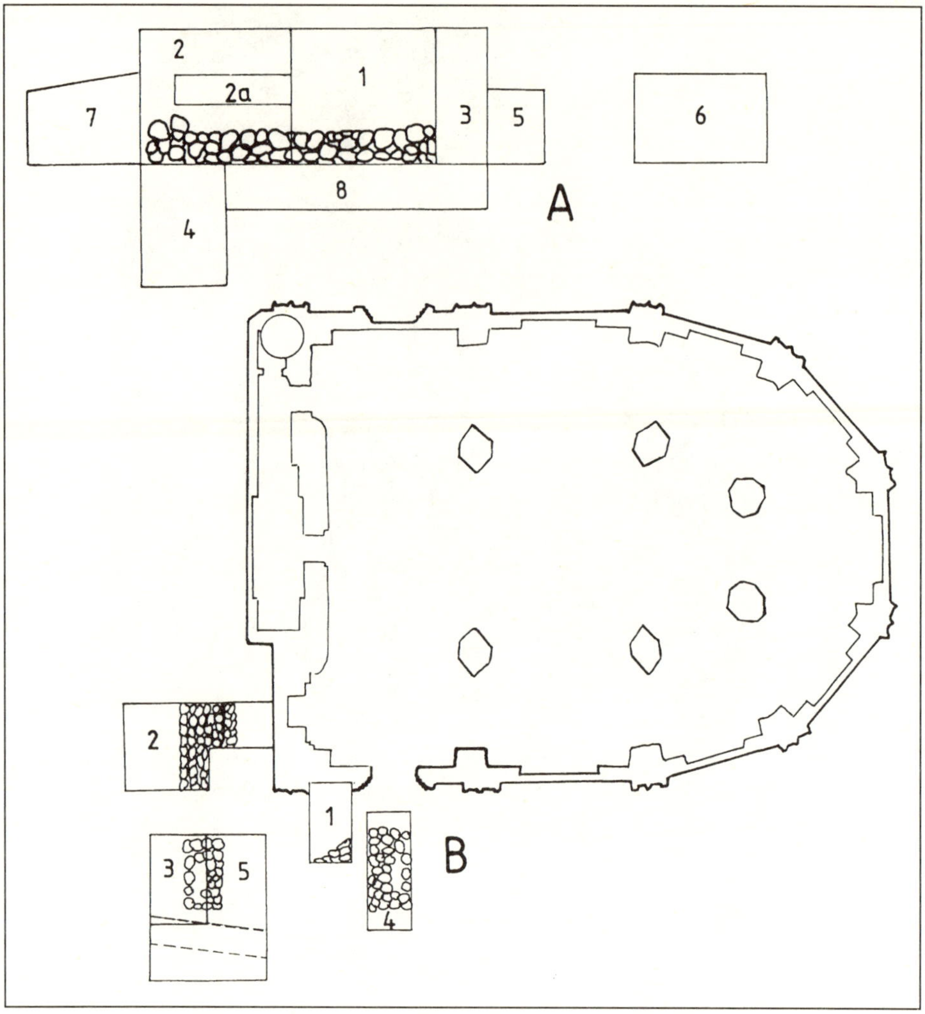

Fig. 4. The outline of the excavated pre-Romanesque foundations. A: research in 1946, B: research in 1999.

temple). With a scintilla of awareness it should be assumed that this layer rather refers to the Romanesque phase of this church. However, we do not have any source data indicating the refurbishing in Romanesque style at our disposal. Nonetheless, indirect claims seem to advocate this supposition. These are as follows: the brick walls were situated on the regular hewed stones (among them there was sandstone ones), whose scratches and the way of treating suggests that it might have been primarily a part of the portal's pier. Furthermore, during the excavation there was found a small fragment of the sandstone-made masonry with a preserved part of the leaf in deep relief. It is possible that it is the remnant of the order of the Romanesque portal or the window casing. It should be reminded that we possess a piece of data concerning the rebuilding of Poznań in 1249, and this date is supposed to designate the time of reparation of the embankments of the duke's part of the stronghold. It was probably at that time when the refurbishment of the stronghold's chapel took place. This claim can only be supported by excavation in the interior of the church. A slight suggestion might be the recorded traces of the demolition of the walls of the pre-Romanesque building (it can be inferred form the presence of the layer of mortar plaster). The next layer containing the lumps of mortar plaster occurred deeper in an excavation from which the 3 meter-wide set of boulders was removed. This layer corresponded stratigraphicaly and constructively to the fragments of the pre-Romanesque foundations. Its interpretation requires further research as well as the character of the cobbles recorded in the southern side of the fragment of the Gothic building has to be determined. The size of the examined parts of the pre-Romanesque foundation, the sort of stones used for its construction, the way of settling, the presence of the white and pink mortar plaster presents one with a vivid correspondence between the foundations of the pre-Romanesque cathedral in Poznań and the palace-sacral complex in Ostrów Lednicki which is situated half way through Poznań and Gniezno.

The research conduced in the vicinity of St Mary's Church supported the claim put forward in literature that in the second half of the 10th century in the duke's part of Poznań stronghold there was a stony *palatium*. Next to this building there supposedly was a palace chapel constituting a complex of the sort known from Ostrów Lednicki. One can also accept the claim that the refurbishment of Poznań stronghold and the erection of the sacral and secular monumental stony architecture in its northern part was connected with Mieszko's the First decision to convert into Christianity and to marry the Czech princess, Dąbrówka.

Around the middle of the 11th century the stronghold in Ostrów Tumski was seriously demolished by the invasion of the Czech ruler, Brzetysław. The devastation mainly affected its northern part. Gall Anonymous writes in his chronicle, "it is at that time, when the Czechs destroyed Gniezno, Poznań and took the body of St. Adalbert... And the mentioned cities remained in neglect for so long that wild animals set their dens in the churches of St. Adalbert the Martyr and St. Peter"[9]. If such miserable fate affected the cathedral, other buildings in its vicinity must have also suffered, though it is not known to what extend. Only on a verge of 11th and 12th centuries was the stronghold rebuilt again in the same form. Its embankments were widened and additionally reinforced with a stony plinth. Ostrów Tumski was inhabited by members of different social strata both secular and ecclesiastic. It was a seat of the bishopric and, from the fist half of the 12th century, the capital of the partitioned duchy. During this time a St. Nicolas parish church was built with and an adjoining graveyard. Having settled the left bank of the Warta in 1253 and built a new duke's castle on the hill into which Przemysł II moved, secular inhabitants left the old stronghold. The ruler gave it to the bishop and since that time it was exclusively a seat of bishopric and Poznań chapter.

[9] *Anonim tzw. Gall. Kronika Polska,* ed. R. Grodecki, Wrocław-Warszawa-Kraków, 1965, pp. 45-46.

Ostrów Tumski was undoubtedly at its prime during the time of Piast monarchy. It was Mieszko I who made this place one of the centers of his reign. It took also a major role in the process of organizing this country. It was an economic, military, and –since the conversion into Christianity– religious center (probably due to becoming in 968 the abode of the first Polish bishop-Jordan). A note about this is included in the bishop Thietmar's chronicle: "the first Poznań bishop-Jordan was incorporated into the rank of those spiritual shepherds"[10]. This note brought about a sever discussion among the medievalists. They pondered upon the legal status of this bishop, his abode, and time and circumstances connected with his arrival to Poland. We leave this question (and the one concerning Jordan being a missionary or diocese bishop[11]) for historians. It is nevertheless possible to determine the place of his supposed abode. According to archeological data the construction of the first cathedral in Poznań is due to the reign of Mieszko I, which makes it the oldest cathedral construction in this domain. It is here where Jordan had its church, which was taken over by bishop Unger in 1000. It is highly probable that at the site of Poznań stronghold there was a castle chapel, which was supposedly funded by Dąbrówka (according to the 13th century Polish Chronicle). This possibility cannot be thoroughly excluded taking into account the fact, that she came to Poland with clergy in 965 to a still pagan country in which there was not a single Christian building. She must have instigated the erection of even the smallest shrine for liturgy. It is now feasible to claim that in the second half of the 10th century the tripartite stronghold complex with the monumental castle (as for its historical period) and two temples took a substantial role in the process of governing the "newly born" state. Also during the reign of Boleslaw the Brave the solidly retrenched castle occupied a very important position, and its importance was put to the test during the war waged with Henry II in 1005. It should be remembered, as was mentioned by Gall Anonymous, that the Bolestaw the Brave's troops included 1300 cuirassiers and 4000 shielded warriors, the biggest unit of warriors (but for the Gniezno unit)[12]. In accordance with the decision made during the Gniezno Convention, Poznań was made the capital of the bishopric, being simultaneously, with other main towns in Great Poland region, the main center of state government. The results of archeological research and written data place both Poznań and Gniezno on the top of the contemporary towns of the early Piast state. The claim might even be put forward that at the end of Mieszko's reign Poznań took the leading role in the Polish state.

---

10 *Kronika Thietmara,* ed. Z. Jedlicki, Poznań, 1953, pp. 72, 74.

11 Ks. M. Banaszak, "Charakter prawny biskupów Jordana i Ungera", *Nasza Przeszłość,* 30, pp. 43-123.

12 *Anonim tzw. Gall. Kronika Polska,* ed. R. Grodecki, Wrocław-Warszawa-Kraków, 1965, p. 27.

RECHERCHES INTERNATIONALES SUR LE CHÂTEAU DE LA TOUR D'ALBON (FRANCE)

TERRY BARRY
Trinity College Dublin. Ireland

JOHNNY DE MEULEMEESTER
Gent University. Belgium

JEAN-MICHEL POISSON
École des Hautes Études. Paris/Lyon, France

This is the conference for the teachers of medieval archaeology and this particular session deals with Specific Research Projects[1]. I am very pleased to talk about the Albon Castle Project and my involvement with it. Then my colleague from the University of Ghent, Johnny De Meulemeester, will talk about the archaeology of the site in some more detail.

Actually, the site itself, *La Tour d'Albon, is* a motte and bailey castle which is very dramatically sited. It is located on top of a spur of land overlooking the Rhône valley, about eighty kilometers south of Lyon.

The research excavation at Albon is a collaborative initiative which involves three partners, the *Unité Mixte de Recherche 5648,* a *CNRS* unit based at the University of Lyon II in France, the Heritage Department of the Walloon Region of Belgium, and the Department of Medieval History in Trinity College Dublin in Ireland. The collaboration stretches also to the University of Lodz in Poland, and the University of Ghent in Belgium and to several other institutions and universities throughout Europe, the Maghreb and the Middle East. So students from Belgium, France, Hungary, Luxembourg, Ireland, Italy, Poland, Spain, Morocco, Syria, Jordan and even Cambodia and the USA have taken part in the excavations. But much of the impetus behind the setting up of this research project came from discussions between two scholars, Jean-Michel Poisson of Lyon and Johnny De Meulemeester from Brussels as a result of their regular attendance at the now famous *Château Gaillard* bi-annual castles conferences all over Europe.

[1] Acknowledgements to Roland Budd for the useful information contained in his report "Summer in the Rhône Valley".

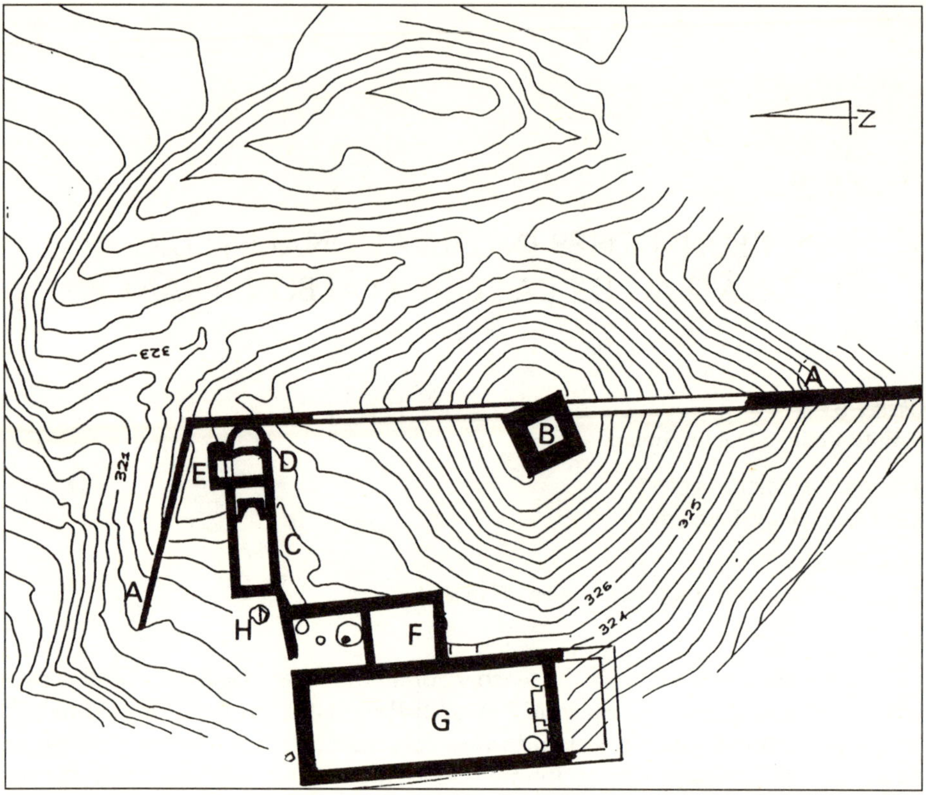

La Tour d'Albon (Drôme, France). Plan général - état auôt 1999. A: mur de courtine; B: le donjon; C: première chapelle castrale, à chevet plat; D: deuxième chapelle à abside en ovale; E: troisième chapelle avec accès par la chapelle latérale; F: bâtiment au sud du mur de terrassement; ultérieurement transformé en étable; G: aula *et* camera*; H: trous de poteaux et silos piriformes.*

Although the project is pursuing a clear research agenda and is one of only two motte and bailey earthwork castles currently being excavated in the whole of France, it also functions excellently well as a training excavation for university students who wish to learn the basic techniques of excavation, recording and surveying. And because Jean-Michel Poisson and Johnny De Meulemeester are co-directors on the site this encourages much discussion among the excavation team about the general approach to the excavation, the excavation methods and also the all important interpretation of the stratigraphic, building and artefactual evidence as it is uncovered. The lack of a strict hierarchy on the site also encourages the development of a good "team work" ethos.

Since the inception of this research project students of Trinity College Dublin have been involved. Indeed, the first undergraduate who started there in 1995, when a prospecting trench was opened across the site, went on to do a Master's degree in archaeology as a research student in University College Cork, before returning to Trinity College to do a PhD with one of the authors, Terry Barry on the origins of Irish tower houses. These are small stone castles dating mainly to the fifteenth and sixteenth centuries, and there are, I would argue, about 7,000 examples of them to be found in Ireland. This would make Ireland the most encastellated country in Europe in the later middle ages. Roland Budd has also taken part in every excavation season at Albon since then, and now acts as a supervisor during the excavation.

This pan-European co-operation has been very beneficial for my undergraduate students generally, especially those who have been doing my Medieval Archaeology Special Subjects in their last two years in Trinity College. This is especially so as they are all essentially history students who are just taking one or, at most, two special subjects in Medieval Archaeology. Because of timetable constraints most of them would have had no prior fieldwork or excavation experience in archaeology, and this is what the training excavation at Albon has provided for them. All together, more than a dozen Trinity students have so far enjoyed the benefits of this essential training in field archaeology; at least one has actually moved on since to a career in professional archaeology. They have also benefited in other ways, such as in broadening their foreign language base by learning French, even if it is archaeological French! Also, they are learning the research excavation techniques as practised in France which is somewhat different from Ireland. Some of my students have also been taught some basic archaeological surveying techniques, as well, which has been very beneficial to their future careers.

This training aspect of the Albon project is especially important for students of archaeology generally as in most European countries, and especially now in the "Celtic Tiger" economy of Ireland, as the very real financial and time constraints of developer-funded excavation make it virtually impossible for contract archaeologists to attempt to instruct or train any beginners. Even for those experienced archaeologists who have taken part in many 'rescue' excavation their involvement in a research excavation such as Albon is obviously very beneficial to them professionally.

From my own viewpoint as a researcher into the archaeology of the castle this cooperative enterprise with several other European institutions has been particularly helpful to me with my own particular interests in the archaeology of the castle, and especially of earthwork castles. For the last few years l have been teaching a new Special Subject in Trinity on the "Archaeology of the medieval castle and military fortifications, 1000-1350". An important part of the first term's work each year is an examination and analysis of the evidence for the origins of the castle in medieval Europe, so the research at Albon has been particularly relevant to this discussion.

In the first few years Irish participation was limited to providing student personnel for the excavation, but more recently Trinity College has been able to help financially with some of the scientific research expenses of the project. It is also hoped that with so many countries involved in the excavation that eventually European Union research money might also assist the excavation.

This year has seen the development of a longer term research strategy in that several of the Albon team are now taking part in other excavations with Johnny De Meulerneester in the south of Belgium near the Luxembourg border, a few weeks before the Albon season. As this has proved so successful, earlier this month Johnny De Meulemeester, who was over in Ireland for the *Ruralia III* conference of medieval rural settlement, also took the opportunity to talk to Dr Kieran O'Conor of the Discovery Programme. As Dr O'Conor is now Director of a major seven year research project for the Discovery Prograrnme on Irish medieval rural settlement, probably concentrating on Gaelic-Irish medieval rural settlement, he will be starting some important excavations in a year or two. So Johnny De Meulemeester has been discussing with him the possibility of the development of a tri-partite scheme whereby the same team of excavators take part in the excavations in France, Belgium and Ireland each year. This will mean that this particular excavation team will each year build up a bank of knowledge and experience in various aspects of European medieval archaeology.

Indeed, the Discovery Programme's expertise in the field of remote sensing and surveying techniques may be very beneficial for these teams of students who have much experience of the continental method of excavation, but who may lack some of the surveying skills necessary to be an "all round" archaeologist. So this developing programme of cooperation that is envisaged will be of great benefit to all the parties engaged in it, and I look forward to reporting on the future development and growth of this cooperative research enterprise to a future ESTMA meeting.

Vers 1030, Guiges, originaire du Vivarais, reçut de l'archevêque de Vienne, les droits comtaux sur la moitié méridionale du comté de Viennois, l'autre échouant au comte de Savoie. Fort de son pouvoir, il étendit très vite son emprise sur le diocèse de Grenoble, puis sur le Grésivaudan. Vers 1040, ce fut de l'empereur germanique lui-même qu'il reçut le Briançonnais. Les Guigues se pareront du titre de comtes d'Albon à partir de 1079. Leur territoire portera le nom de Dauphiné en 1293 et deviendra français en 1349. A partir du château dynastique de "La Tour d'Albon" dominant la vallée du Rhône, les comtes d'Albon ont ainsi pu étendre leurs possessions vers l'est jusqu'à la crête des Alpes.

La Tour d'Albon occupe un emplacement remarquable pour plusieurs raisons. Il s'agit d'abord d'un point stratégique de premier ordre. En effet, juchée à 336 mètres d'altitude sur l'extrémité d'une colline allongée qui limite au sud la plaine de la Valloire à son débouché sur la vallée du Rhône, cette belle tour médiévale domine un vaste territoire de terres alluviales. En outre, par temps clair, on découvre de là aussi bien les monts du Vivarais à l'ouest que les Alpes du côté opposé. Mais qui dit point de vue dit aussi point de mire: il ne faut pas négliger la fonction symbolique qu'a pu revêtir ce site visible d'aussi loin.

Le château de la Tour d'Albon se présente actuellement sous forme d'une motte castrale, séparée du plateau par un profond fossé de plus d'une dizaine de mètres et par un rempart extérieur massif. Sur le tertre se trouve la "Tour d'Albon"; il s'agit d'un donjon carré de près de 7,50 mètres de côté. On distingue à l'intérieur comme à l'extérieur, trois niveaux: le rez-dechaussée actuel et deux étages. Sur chacun d'eux s'ouvraient des meurtrières ou des fenêtres étroites. Au premier étage, du côté sud-est, une ouverture en plein cintre marque une porte donnant accès au bâtiment.

Adossée au pied du tertre, est implantée une basse-cour qui n'est pas séparée de la motte par un fossé. Sa superficie est relativernent restreinte et ne pouvait donner place qu'à un nombre limité de constructions.

Les fouilles, toujours en cours, se sont concentrées sur cette basse-cour. Elles ont dégagé plusieurs constructions appartenant à différentes époques. Il s'agit de structures en bois, d'une chapelle castrale, d'une grande *aula* et d'une grande dépendance qui ont chacune connu diverses périodes de construction. Ces ensembles montrent assurément que la motte castrale ne représente que la phase ultime de l'occupation médiévale du site.

PHASE I

Vers l'an 1000 une petite chapelle castrale, à chevet plat, occupait la partie septentrionale du site. Elle fut construite en deux phases distinctes: le choeur semi-circulaire et le prernier mètre de la nef sont construits en blocs de molasse, au moins pour le parement, tandis que le restes des murs de la nef emploient en majorité des moellons de granite. Pour l'instant, on n'a pas pu déterminer si les murs de la nef représentent une réfection ou s'ils remplacent un état de construction avec des pans de bois. Au total, la chapelle mesmait quelques 12 m sur 6 m *extra muros*. Son mur occidental et surtout son angle nord-ouest furent implantés sur la pente naturelle plus raide ce qui nécessitait des fondations plus profondes.

A cette même époque appartiennent un certain nombre de trous de poteaux, restes d'installations en bois, pour l'instant en cours de fouilles et non encore déterminées. Il vont de pair avec une série de grands silos piriformes creusés dans la moraine. Pour l'instant 6 exemplaires ont été reconnus, dont 4 sont implantés sur un alignement à la base d'une des pentes naturelles du site.

Notons que les constructions en bois et les silos, dont l'implantation tient nettement compte du terrain naturel, ne prennent pas la même orientation que la chapelle qui elle a été en partie creusée dans la pente naturelle. D'ailleurs, l'emplacement d'un des silos devant le mur oriental de la nef, suggère que la chapelle, ou au moins la construction de la nef, ne représente pas le premier stade d'occupation du site, à moins que la nef originale n'ait été plus courte.

Il ne faut pas exclure que, sous la motte, d'autres bâtiments appartenant à cette époque complètent le bâti du site. L'ensemble était défendu par un rempart et un fossé extérieur comme le montre une coupe à travers le rempart extérieur ultérieur.

PHASE II

Au XIIe siècle le chœur de cette chapelle fut arasé et remplacé par un édifice plus long à abside en ovale qui allongeait le bâtiment d'environ 6 m vers l'est. Le mur oriental de cet édifice a été seulement retrouvé en négatif. Elle fut complétée, au nord, par une chapelle latérale à absidiole. Par contre, ses murs latéraux construits en blocs de molasse bien taillés, viennent s'appuyer sur les murs de la nef de la chapelle précédente. Dans le mur méridional une porte de quelque 150 cm de largeur permettait de sortir de la nouvelle nef, quoique pour atteindre le plateau, il fallait traverser un passage creusé dans le terrain naturel. Dans l'arrondi sud-est de l'abside fut retrouvé un bassin d'évacuation des eaux d'un lavabo liturgique. Les couches d'occupation ont procuré du mobilier des XIe et XIIe siècles.

Considérant que l'apogée des Guigues comme seigneurs d'Albon se situe au XIIe siècle, il est compréhensible que l'agrandissement de la chapelle castrale va de pair avec la construction d'une grande *aula* d'un type commun aux grandes résidences des princes territoriaux de l'empire germanique. Mais, il n'a pas encore été établi lequel des deux vient d'abord. Il est clair que l'*aula* se greffe sur l'orientation de la chapelle avec laquelle elle est construite à angle droit. Le bâtiment se compose de l'*aula* proprement dite et de la *camera* seigneuriale; la première couvre une surface *intra muros* d'environ 23 m sur 9 m; pour une même largeur, la *camera* prolonge le bâtiment probablement sur quelque 6 m Pour construire un bâtiment d'une telle envergure, les constructeurs devaient même creuser la pente naturelle pour permettre l'implantation de la *camera.* L'ensemble fut construit en couches horizontales régulières de galets et parementé de beaux blocs de molasse. Un texte de 1406 nous apprend que le bâtiment disposait de deux étages, chaque fois avec salle et chambre privée. A l'étage, l'*aula* était éclairée par 4 grandes fenêtres qui s'ouvraient sur la vallée du Rhône. Au rez-de-chaussée, la salle disposait d'une grande cheminée sur le mur méridional; à côté de la cheminée, une porte donnait accès à la *camera.* Le bâtiment est en cours de fouilles.

A cette époque le site ne fut plus protégé par un rempart de terre; bien que ce dernier fut conservé, la défense du site devenu prestigieux fut augmenté par 1'érection d'un mur de courtine construit en couches alternées de galets et de blocs de molasse. Il n'est pas encore certain si ce mur cernait déjà le bourg castral.

PHASE III

Dans un stade suivant, le mur oriental de l'abside de la chapelle et le mur méridional de la chapelle latérale furent démolis pour permettre la construction d'une nouvelle chapelle. A hauteur de l'ancien arc triomphal, le mur de chaînage fut élargi pour constituer un mur de façade; en effet, la nouvelle chapelle limite le bâtiment liturgique à une longueur de quelques 8 m. La chapelle latérale fut conservée, mais son mur septentrional fut percé pour permettre l'implantation d'une porte qui par une marche donnait accès à la nouvelle chapelle. Cette modification de l'entrée fut nécessaire puisque la porte primitive se situait maintenant en dehors de la chapelle. D'ailleurs, dans cette nouvelle phase de construction, la porte fut rétrécie à 1 m de largeur et, du côté du plateau, elle donnait maintenant accès à un bâtiment à fonction artisanale occupé, entre autre, par un malaxeur à mortier. Cette phase de remodelage du site se situe encore au XIIIe siècle si on suit la fréquentation et l'abandon de la zone artisanale dans la partie ouest du bâtiment de la chapelle (C-14, monnaie, céramique).

PHASE IV

Encore au XIIIe siècle, on érigea la motte et le donjon qui rappelle des caractéristiques architecturales du XIIe siècle, mais qui, dans cette région, sont encore communes au XIIIe siècle. Le tertre de la motte couvrit en partie la courtine. Au pied de la motte - et de ce qui restait apparent de la courtine, un profond fossé fut creusé; les terres servirent à augmenter le volume du premier rempart de terre, peut-être même celui du tertre. Le nouvel ensemble barrait l'accès au site du côté du plateau. Cette transformation fondamentale venait à un moment où les seigneurs d'Albon avaient quitté leur site dynastique pour d'autres résidences, comme Grenoble. Le site reçut plus une fonction de contrôle et d'utilité que de résidence. Déjà la réduction de l'édifice religieux au profit d'un bâtiment utilitaire marqua le début de cette évolution. Elle sera complétée par la construction d'un mur de terrassement qui joint l'angle sud-ouest de la chapelle/atelier et l'angle nord-est de l'*aula* et d'un bâtiment utilitaire au sud de ce mur; une porte fut percée dans le muret de jonction pour permettre l'entrée à cette nouvelle installation contre laquelle s'appuient les remblais de l'emmottement. Ce bâtiment, qui couvre une surface intérieure d'environ 14 m sur 5 m, s'appuie contre le mur oriental de l'*aula.* L'intérieur est divisé, au milieu, en deux nefs longitudinales par des poteaux reposants sur des grandes pierres posées dans les trous de poteaux; il s'agit sans aucun doute des poteaux qui supportaient la poutre faîtière. La construction du muret de terrassement est datée du XIIIe siècle par de la céramique "très décore" prise dans sa maçonnerie. Les couches d'occupation du batiment sont datées du XIVe siècle.

PHASE V

Le compte rendu de visite de 1406 nous instruit sur l'évolution ultérieure. Ainsi, nous s'avons que la construction, à l'est de l'*aula,* fut transformée en étable. A cette occasion, la surface fut partagée en deux parties égales dans le sens nord-sud par la construction d'un mur de refend qui traverse les couches d'occupation du XIVe siècle. Dans l'*aula,* les murs furent réparés et, à part pour les fondations, le mur séparant *aula* et *camera* fut complètement refait.

PHASE VI

Finalement, le château est abandonné à partir du XVIe siècle; pendant les XVIIe/XVIIIe siècles, il servira comme carrière de récupération de matériaux. Seul le donjon survivra.

CONCLUSION

En guise de conclusion nous pouvons dire que le prograrnme de la Tour d'Albon tourne autour de deux pôles, les buts éducatifs et les buts scientifiques. Pour les premiers nous sommes convaincus de l'intérêt que ce programme international présente pour les étudiants. En ce qui concerne l'aspect scientifique, personne ne doute de l'importance du site d'Albon pour nos connaissances de l'évolution d'un site dynastique dans cette partie de l'Europe, mais nous sommes aussi très conscients qu'il faudra encore plusieurs campagnes de fouilles avant que les résultats présentés obtienent un caractère définitif.

MEDIEVAL FORTIFICATIONS IN THE PROVINCE OF SEVILLE (ANDALUCÍA, SPAIN)

MAGDALENA VALOR PIECHOTTA
University of Seville (Spain)

Our knowledge of Medieval fortifications in the Iberian peninsula is surprisingly poor. As regards southern Spain, or Andalusia, the existing studies and publications may be described as scarce. Only after 1986 did research groups, financed by the regional government or foreign institutions like the Casa de Velázquez (C.N.R.S., France), enable archaeological projects related with fortification and territory to be set up.

Since 1989, the Medieval History Department of Seville University has been developing a research project[1] supported by the Andalusian Education Department (Consejería de Educación y Ciencia) and the Andalusian Culture Department (Consejería de Cultura-Dirección General de Bienes Culturales), both of which form part of the regional government (Junta de Andalucía).

---

1 M. Valor Piechotta, S. Rodríguez Guzmán, "Las fortificaciones medievales en el Aljarafe sevillano", *Anuario Arqueológico de Andalucía/1991,* 1993, II, pp. 363-373. M. Valor Piechotta, "La poliorcética medieval en el Reino de Sevilla", *Investigaciones Arqueológicas en Andalucía,* Huelva, 1993, pp. 747-754. "Una aproximación a la arquitectura militar de la segunda mitad del siglo XIII", *IV Congreso de Arqueología Medieval Española,* Alicante, 1994, II, pp. 415-422. "Las fortificaciones medievales en el reino de Sevilla", *Arqueología en el entorno del Bajo Guadiana,* Huelva, 1994, pp. 645-655. M. Valor, N. Casquete de Prado, "El castillo de Cumbres Mayores (Huelva). Una aproximación a la arquitectura militar de la segunda mitad del siglo XIII", *Historia, Instituciones y Documentos,* 1994, 21, pp. 473-499. M. Valor, "Avance sobre los resultados de la prospección arqueológica de superficie de las fortificaciones medievales de la Vega de Sevilla. Campaña 1993", *Anuario Arqueológico de Andalucía/1993,* 1997, II, pp. 159-169. "Las fortificaciones de la Banda Gallega: algunos ejemplos de las provincias de Huelva y Badajoz y del Alemtejo portugués", *La fortaleza medieval. Realidad y símbolo. Actas de la XV Asamblea General de la Sociedad Española de Estudios Medievales,* Murcia, 1998, pp. 91-108. "Las defensas de Carmona", *Archivo Hispalense,* 1997, LXXX, pp. 597-635. M. Valor, J. López, N. Casquete de Prado, "Intervención Arqueológica de Apoyo a la restauración en el Proyecto *Entorno del Castillo de Cortegana (Huelva)*", *Anuario Arqueológico de Andalucía/1995* (en prensa). M. Valor, "Approximation à les fortifications d'al-Andalus pendant le Haut Moyen Age", *III Symposium for Teachers of Medieval Archaeology,* Caen (Normandía, Francia), 1996, Caen, 1999, pp. 177-200. "Las fortificaciones medievales en la bailía de Setefilla (Sevilla)", *I Congreso de Castellología Ibérica (Aguilar de Campoo. 1994),* Palencia, 1998, pp. 723-760. *Castillo de Cote. Intervención Arqueológica de Urgencia,* Memoria de Excavación depositada en 1999 en la Delegación Provincial de Cultura de Sevilla. M. Valor Piechotta et alii, "El proyecto de investigación: entorno del castillo de Cote", *Actas de las III Jornadas de temas Moronenses,* Morón de la Frontera, 1998, pp. 15-36.

In this project, the first aim was to draw up an inventory of fortifications, including city walls, castles and towers. This was fundamental because of the limited number of previous publications on this subject. Therefore, our starting point was the analysis and study of each of the single cases still remaining. The research method we have followed is that of archaeological survey, which involves:

1) The study of written sources and general literature in this province.
2) An inventory of graphic documents: maps, plans, photos, etc.
3) Survey and analysis of each example.
4) Search for and study of similarities in the Iberian peninsula and the Magreb.

One of the first decisions to be made was the definition of the territorial limits of this inventory. If we use historical criteria, we would see completely different limits between the province which exists now (defined in 1833) and the one which dates from the Middle Ages. However, if we go back to the Medieval limits of Seville's territory, we also find many changes. If we simplified this reality, we could refer to two main periods, namely:

- The Muslim, or Andalusí period.
- The Medieval Christian period, defined after 1255.

Finally, we decided to use the present-day limits for our investigation. Therefore, we are dealing with an area of 1.400.043 hectares, which has to be divided into smaller areas, using criteria based on the division made by the Spanish Ministry of Agriculture[2]. The districts, called comarcas, are seven in all, namely: Sierra Norte, Vega, Aljarafe, Marismas, Campiña, Sierra Sur and Sierra de Estepa (Fig. 1). These units are essentially based on data derived from physical geography, which is also a logical division in the historical sense.

The Province of Seville, according to the *Inventory of European Cultural Heritage (Inventario de Patrimonio Cultural Europeo*[3] or I.P.C.E), has a total of 84 fortifications in its register: 12 city walls, 48 castles, 22 towers and 2 fortified manors (Fig. 2).

In spite of the fact that such a large number of Medieval fortifications in Seville are listed, the inventory remains incomplete. Nevertheless, this publication can be regarded as a useful starting point for our research, The initial ob-

[2] Ministerio de Agricultura, Pesca y Alimentación. Consejería de Agricultura y Pesca de la Junta de Andalucía, *Mapa de Cultivos y Aprovechamientos de la Provincia de Sevilla,* Madrid, 1986.

[3] Ministerio de Educación y Ciencia, *Inventario de Patrimonio Cultural Europeo. España. Monumentos de Arquitectura Militar,* Madrid, 1968.

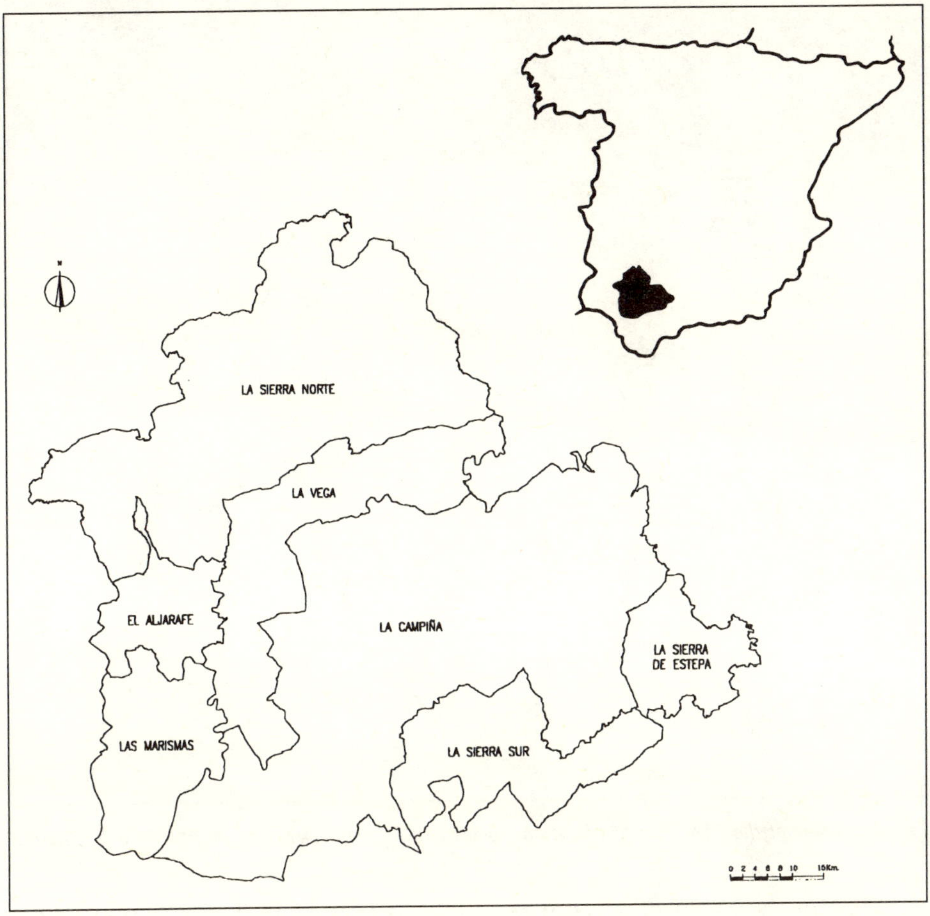

Fig. 1. The province of Seville, its location in the Iberian peninsula and its division into agrarian areas.

jective of this study, therefore, is the working out, correction and completion of this corpus.

Two factors, which constantly and decisively determine Medieval military buildings in this geographical area, must be taken into account previously, namely:

1) The fixing of a **chronological framework** to which our research will be circumscribed. This task must be regarded as an essential premise. The two main periods in question are:

- Fortifications between 711 (Muslim Conquest) and 1009 (end of Omeyyad reign).
- From 1000 to 1500.

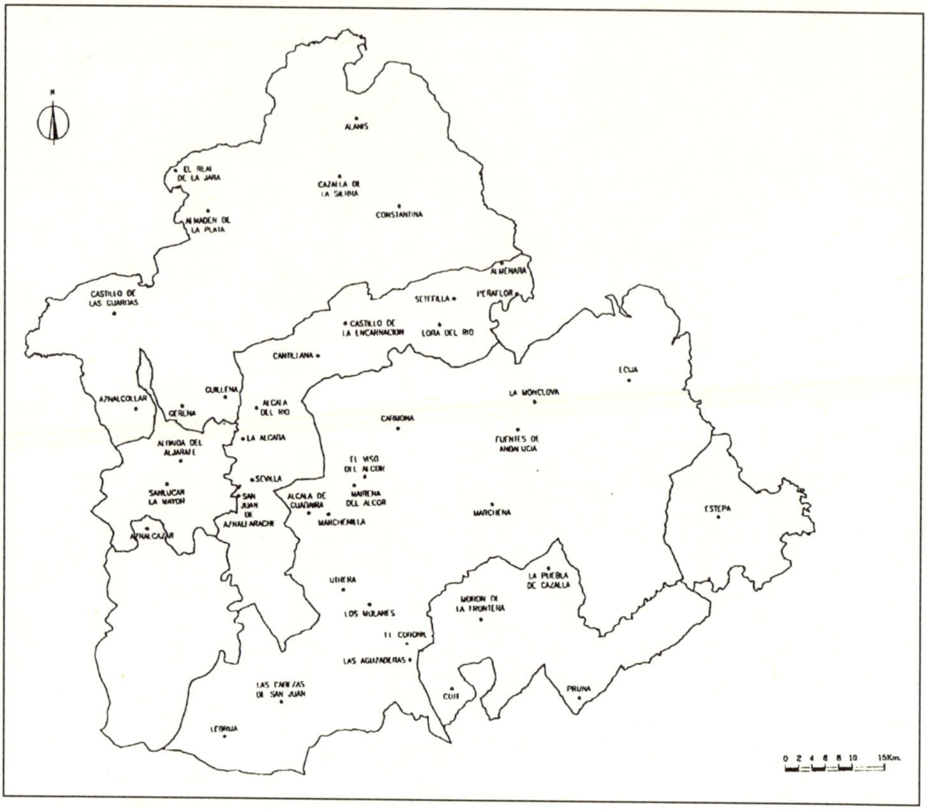

Fig. 2. Some of the Medieval fortifications located in different agrarian areas (M. Valor, 2001).

Most of the fortifications still remaining belong to the latter period. There is no doubt that fortifications were used before, but practically no traces of any from the early Middle Ages are to be seen now.

2) **The geographical factor** is also of great relevance. If a map of the Province of Seville is studied in depth, three well-defined areas will be differentiated:

- The Northern area: Sierra Morena.
- The Central Area: The Guadalquivir Valley.
- The Southern Area: Sierra Subbética.

Each area has its own logic-determining factors. For instance, the central area is the most densely populated, and, at times, no break in continuity can be found between Prehistory and the present time. On the other hand, the mountainous areas are thinly populated, although some fortified settlements of a certain significance can be found. In the case of Sierra Morena, these are connected to mining activities.

On analysing this splendid heritage from the chronological point of view, the following conclusions can be drawn:

1. FORTIFICATIONS UP TO THE END OF THE FIRST MILLENNIUM

We are dealing with different political situations in al-Andalus: pre-Omeyyad period and Omeyyads. Few remains belonging to these periods can be found. Regarding the province as a whole, the following cases can be confirmed:

1.1. Previous fortifications, which in some cases were re-used. These pre-Islamic fortifications have Prehistoric origins in certain cases, such as Setefilla castle (Lora del Río); in other cases, the origin could be Roman, such as Alcalá del Río. The same situation could apply to city walls, such as those found in Écija, Carmona or pre-Almohad Seville.

1.2. Ex-novo fortifications. There are already two examples, but only archaeological excavation could find more cases that evidently must exist.

The foundational enclosure of the Alcazár of Seville, built during the Omeyyade Emirate. It is a building which evidently belongs to the Syrian tradition, not only because of its layout, but also because of its general conception. The building materials used are stone ashlars, most of which are re-used from Roman buildings. It consists of a square, flanked by slightly protruding small towers, which are evenly distributed along the four flanks, with four larger corner towers (Fig. 3).

In Carmona, we find a few remains of Omeyyad fortifications in the Alcazár and in the city walls.

Many more fortifications from these centuries must exist, but we need data provided by archaeological excavations.

2. FORTIFICATIONS BETWEEN 1000 AND 1500

This is a lengthy period with a complicated development, for the following reasons:

- Many buildings still exist.
- The written sources are particularly abundant, especially in the Late Medieval centuries.
- The cultural change from a Muslim to a Christian civilization.

2.1. Andalusí Fortifications

We are dealing here with a long period, extending from the 11th century (1009= to the 13th [1236 or 1248]). Two different phases can be identified:

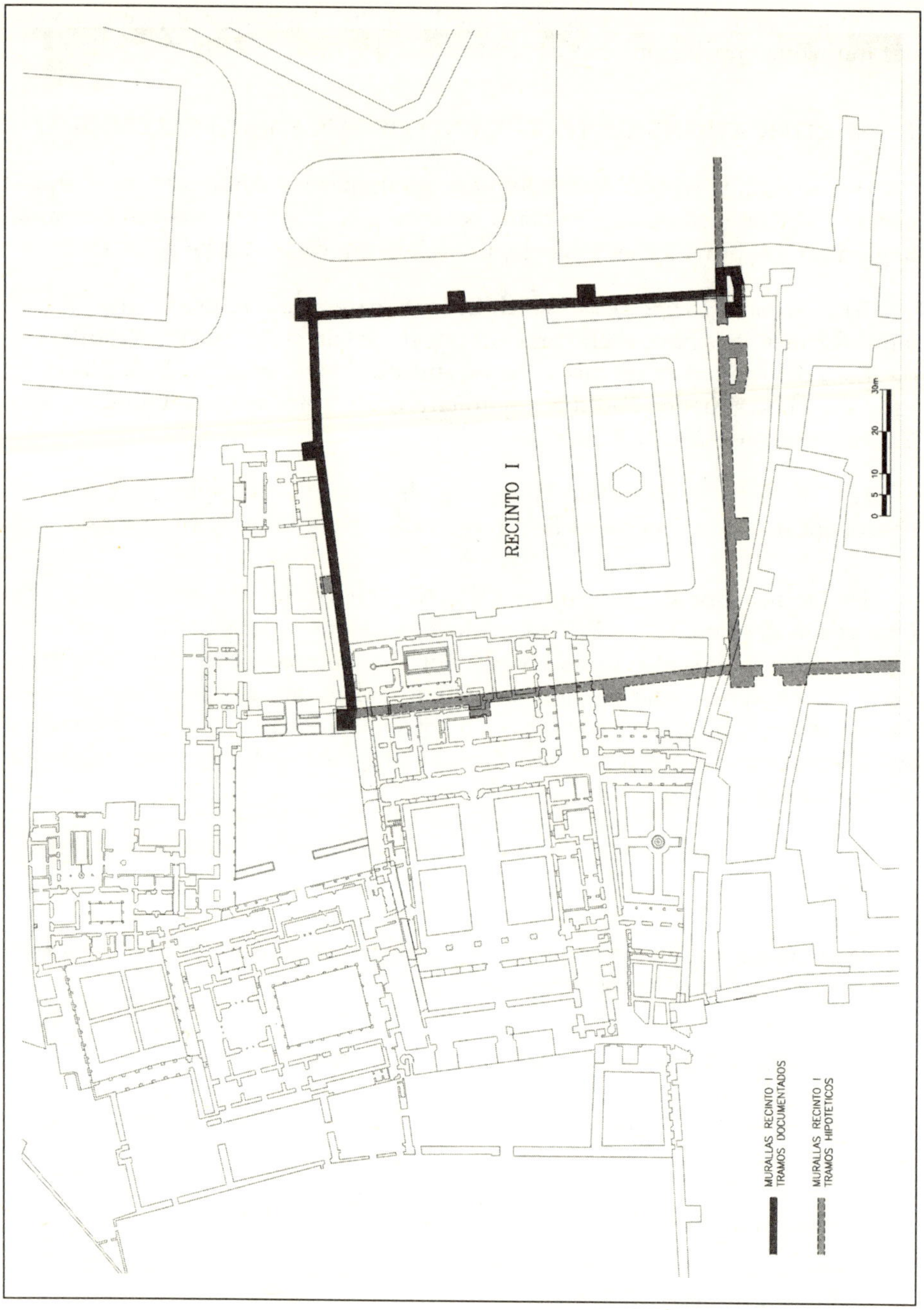

Fig. 3. First urban castle of Seville. From M. Tabales, "Investigaciones en el Alcázar de Sevilla. Apuntes sobre evolución constructiva y espacial", Apuntes del Alcázar de Sevilla, *2000, nº 1, pp. 13-45.*

A) *The 11th century until the first half of the 12th century; in political terms the Taifa kingdoms and Almoravid kingdom.* The 11th century is the most important phase when the territory of al-Andalus was divided into many small kingdoms. This situation brought about substantial changes in settlement, as well as a renovation of old fortifications, and the construction of new ones on hilltops. This process is known to the Italians as *incastellamento.* After this, the castles were to be a permanent characteristic of rural settlement in al-Andalus.

Not enough archaeological research has been done in order to determine the impact of this century, although hopefully, in a few years' time, we will be better equipped to understand this aspect, not only for castles, but also for city walls.

An example dated in this period is a castle called Cote (Montellano) in the south of Seville, which was excavated by a team from Seville University in 1998. It is a small rectangular castle adapted to the top of a mountain, with a splendid overview of the surrounding territory. The castle and a cistern (43 m^3) were built in the 11th century: the Taifa period (Fig. 4).

The Almoravids dominated al-Andalus for half a century (57 years, between 1090 and 1147). At present, we can not identify any fortifications from this period in the Seville area, but we know, through the written sources, that some buildings were renovated, namely the case of the city of Seville.

B) *Mid-12th century (1147) until mid-13th century (1248): the Almohad empire.* Intense building activity took place during this period, especially between 1171 and the Christian conquest of the territory between 1240 and 1248. In these years, the Almohads and the 3rd Taifa kingdoms built significant fortifications,

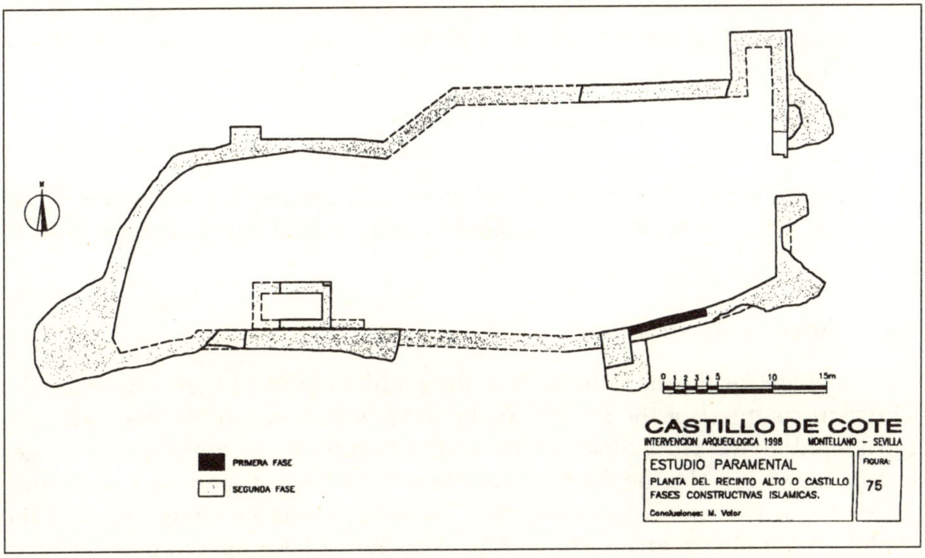

Fig. 4. Islamic Cote castle, enclosure and cistern (M. Valor, 1998).

which were designed to defend the frontiers, not only in a linear way, but also in depth (roads, navigable rivers, and fertile valleys). Likewise, real castle walls were also built for the protection of relevant urban centres. The clearest example of this is the city wall of Seville (Fig. 5), which at that time was the capital city of the Almohad Caliphate in al-Andalus.

Many ex-novo examples still exist. The following categories can be discerned:

- Small castles, intended as itinerary castles, located on river banks or mountain passes (Plate 1).
- Castles with a walled village. In Arabic they are known as a *hisn* with an *al-qasar,* and are also located on main communication routes and in fertile valleys (Fig. 6).
- City walls, ex-novo ramparts in urban centres with an earlier origin. The specific characteristic of this type is their huge size, which is the case of Seville (Plate 2).

All these fortifications have a common building design. *Tabiya* (a kind of mortar) is the building material mainly used (Plate 3). Regarding their structure, clear differences can be found between fortifications located in rural areas and city walls; the latter are much more elaborate and effective.

Examples of fortifications which still exist from this period are:

- City walls: Seville, Écija, Marchena and (partially) Carmona.
- Castles: Cantillana, Lora del Río, Peñaflor, Almenara (Peñaflor); La Encarnación (Villanueva del Río and Minas), Sanlúcar la Mayor, Alcalá de Guadaria.
- Towers: a few examples around Seville.

It can be stated that fortifications were built around the important urban centre, in the vicinity of the Guadalquivir river and in fertile valleys close to Seville.

2.2. Christian Fortifications

These are fortifications built from the middle of the 13th century, when the Christian conquest of the lower Guadalquivir valley began, to 1500, which is considered as the chronological end of the Middle Ages. Significant changes in typology may also be found throughout this lengthy period, which comprises about two and a half centuries. Likewise, it can be confirmed that the evolution of military architecture occurs somewhat later than in other parts of Europe.

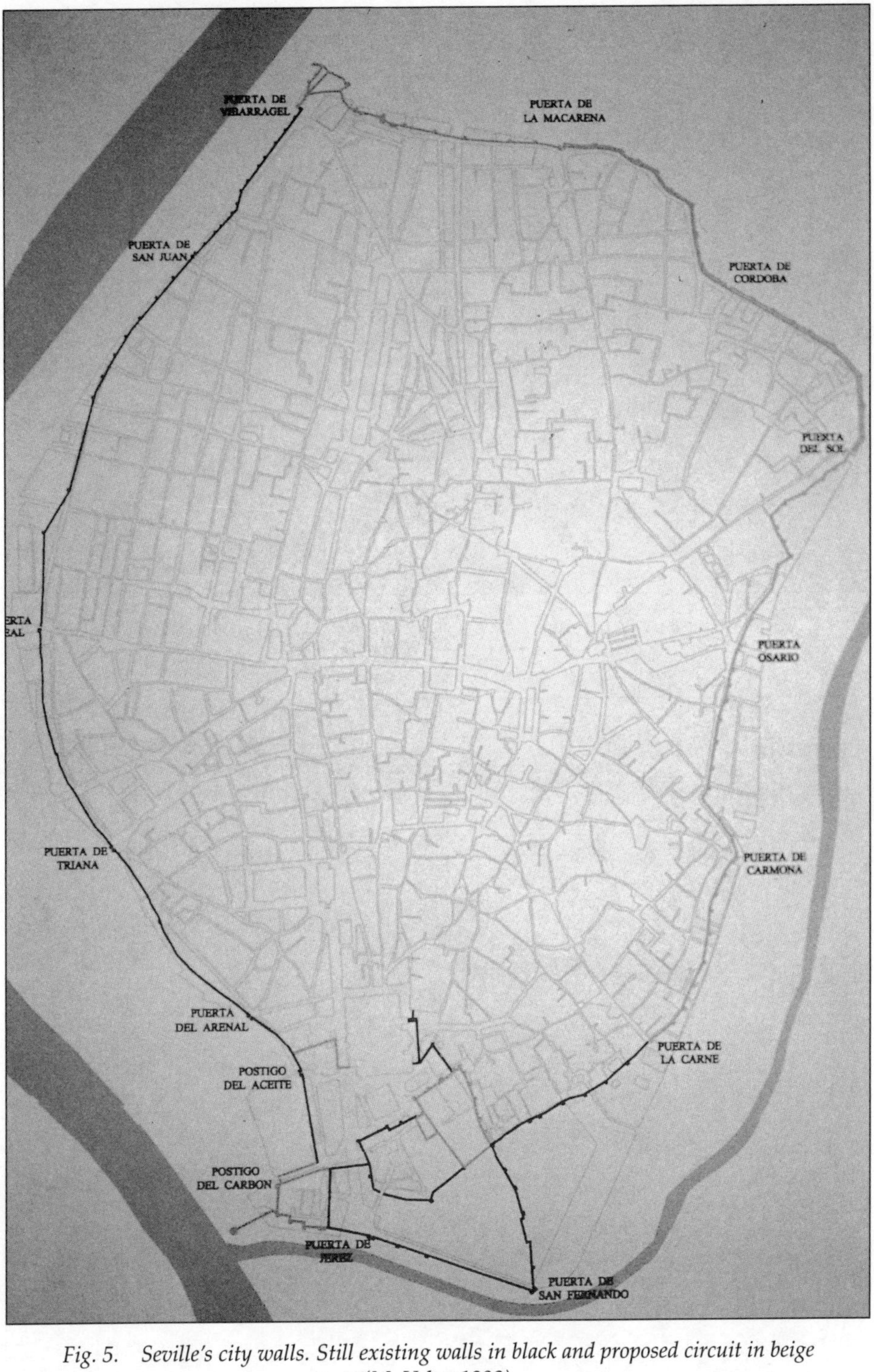

Fig. 5. Seville's city walls. Still existing walls in black and proposed circuit in beige (M. Valor, 1999).

Plate 1. Itinerary castle of Lora del Río. Pre-islamic settlement with preserved Almohad walls (M. Valor, 1994).

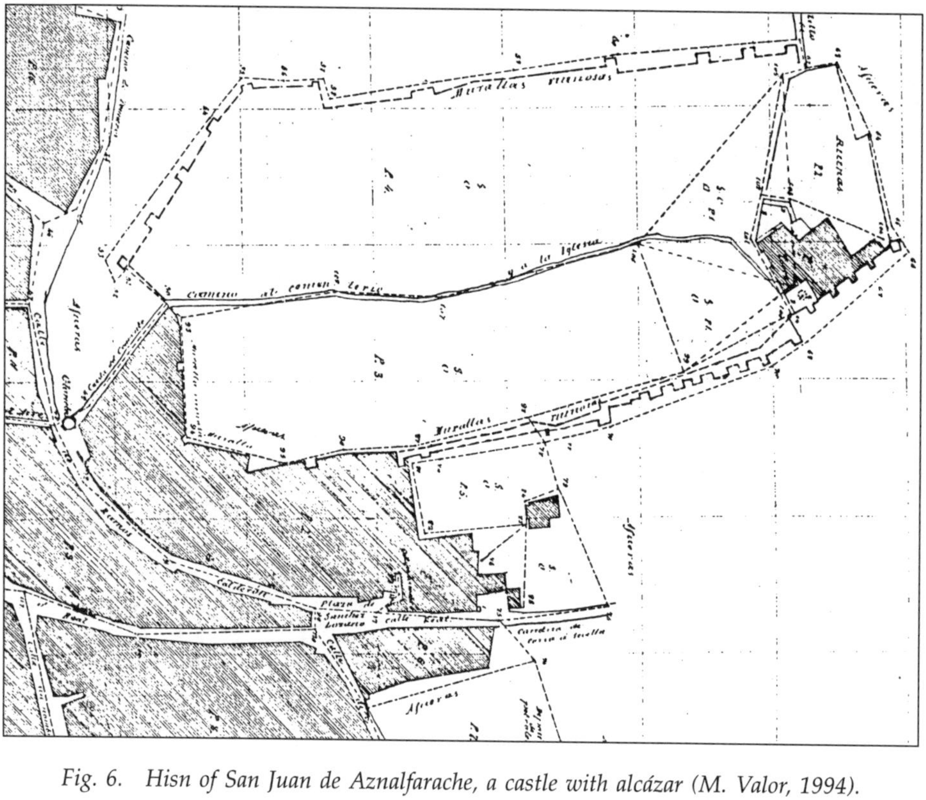

Fig. 6. Hisn of San Juan de Aznalfarache, a castle with alcázar (M. Valor, 1994).

Plate 2. Two towers of Seville's alcázar: The Silver and the Gold Towers (Carlos Ortega, 1998).

Plate 3. Tower made in tabiya, in the south of Seville city (M. Valor, 1998).

It was during this period when most of the fortifications were built, probably for an obvious reason, as follows:

In the Andalusí period, a great distance had separated this territory from the Christian border. Therefore, fortifications were only built in major cities of the region, as well as in places defending communication routes, and those located in important economic areas, such as mining areas or fertile valleys.

This situation altered in the Castilian period, and the lower Guadalquivir valley became a frontier area with the kingdoms of Granada and Portugal. Both borders conformed to natural geographical accidence, such as the Baetic mountain range in the former case and the Sierra Morena in the latter. The fact that the lower Guadalquivir valley was a borderland led to the rebuilding of existing fortifications, to which so many new features were added that the Islamic origin sometimes became unrecognisable. On the other hand, the ex-novo building of many castles made it possible for areas which had hitherto remained empty to be filled up. This process, stretching from the end of the 13th century to the middle of the 14th, was the result of an initiative taken by kings and military orders, and was to bring about the emergence of a most varied typology of fortifications. In the 14th century, the nobility was to take the initiative. Fortifications were also built after this date, but were within the framework of a completely different historical situation. During the last third of the 15th century, the reinforcement of some old fortifications or the building of new ones was the result of the continual struggles which occurred between different factions of the nobility. These new buildings or reinforcements are halfway between Medieval fortifications and bastions.

Plate 4. Cote dojon, constructed in the centre of the Islamic castle (M. Valor, 1997).

A) *The second half of the 13th century.* This is a very interesting period, during which the co-existence of completely different building styles has been demonstrated[4]. Such styles range from the Gothic, which may be found in fortifications constructed by the Castilian royal family (Plate 4) to fortifications within the Almohad tradition (Plate 5). This coexistence of different building styles after the Christian conquest is a relevant aspect which, logically, can be seen much more clearly in religious architecture. The mosques, which were transformed into churches, are good examples of this.

B) *From the second quarter of the 14th century to the middle of the 15th century.* The lower Guadalquivir area near the border with the Kingdom of Granada was re-organized specifically in the course of the 14th century. This process is not specified in any explicit project, but, nonetheless, if we analyse the colonisation charters which were granted to noblemen and peasants, we find that a series of advantages were systematically offered to them, provided they fulfilled their specific obligations of colonizing and defending the lands conceded to them.

As a result of the surveys carried out, we have found that these fortifications have many architectural features in common, such as the building design, the use of tabiya, and the type of towers –much larger than before– with a residential function. There are many examples in existence, such as Aguza-

4 M. Valor Piechotta, "Una aproximación a la arquitectura militar de la segunda mitad del siglo XIII", *IV Congreso de Arqueología Medieval Española,* Alicante, 1994, II, pp. 415-422.

Plate 5. Albaida del Aljarafe tower, built by a son of the conqueror, king Fernando III (M. Valor, 1992).

deras Castle (Plate 6), and Mairena del Alcor Castle (Fig. 7). Both of these examples are newly-built castles, but there are also examples of pre-existent fortifications which were re-built, which is the case of Setefilla Castle in Lora del Río (Fig. 8).

C) *The second half of the 15th century.* This building period may be defined well by means of two features:

- The abundance of written sources, as opposed to previous stages.
- Fortifications were built in a specific style, that of a military architecture halfway between Medieval fortifications and bastions. Battlements with different kinds of gun loops can be found. The castle of Mairena del Alcor is a good example of this (Plate 6).

To conclude, we need archaeological excavations in order to as certain aspects such as continuity, evolution, inside-wall structures, and an archaeological survey in order to establish the territorial limits, the relationship between castles and villages (alquerías), the environment and its changes during the Middle Ages, etc. At present, we can trace a picture of the heritage still existing, as well as its condition and its stages of conservation.

Plate 6. Las Aguzaderas castle in El Coronil (M. Valor, 1994).

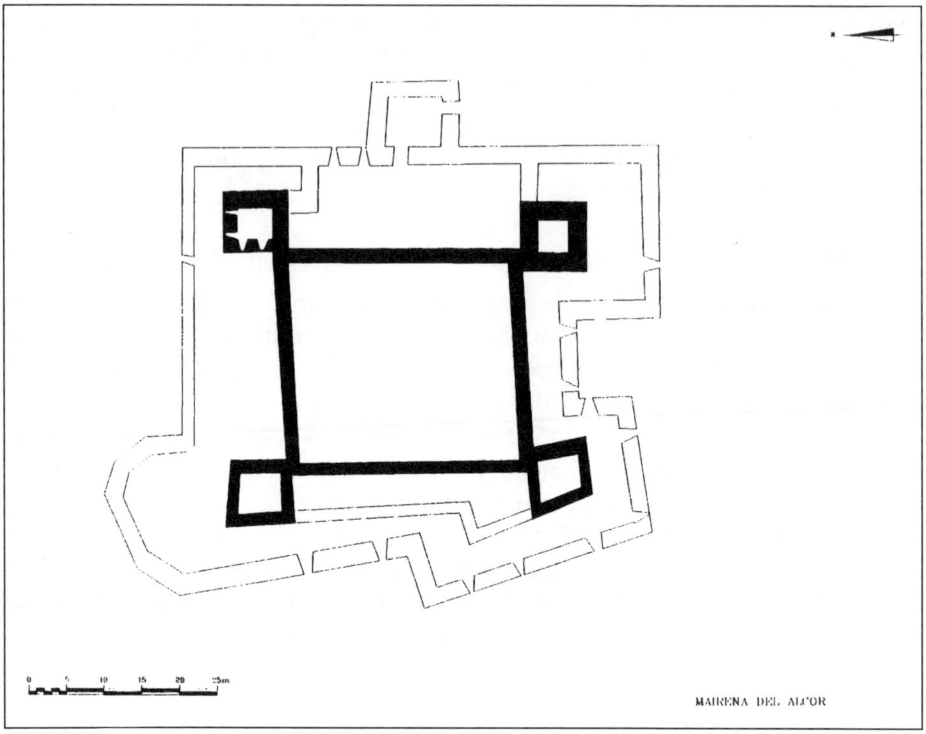

Fig. 7. Mairena del Alcor castle. In black outer-wall dating from the 15th century; in white the 14th century castle (M. Valor, 1994).

Plate 7. Mairena del Alcor outer wall, dating from the 15th century.

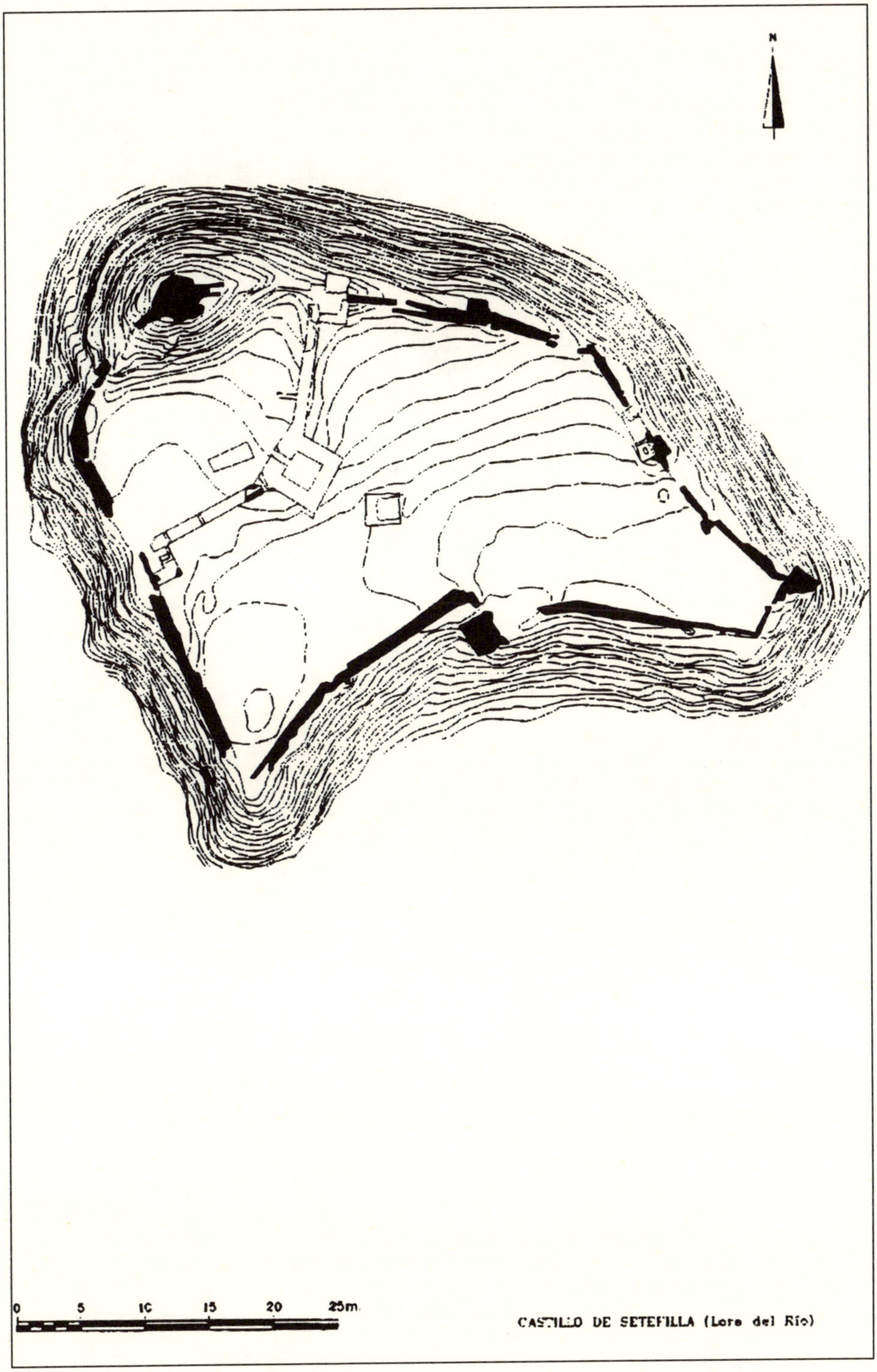

Fig. 8. Setefilla castle. In white the 14th century inner-wall, in black the pre-Christian fortification (M. Valor).

WORK PLAN

WEDNESDAY 29TH SEPTEMBER

16.00-19.00: Arrival. Registration at the Department of Medieval History.

19.30: Reception. *Fundición Real. Casa de la Moneda.*

THURSDAY 30TH SEPTEMBER
(Fundición Real, Casa de la Moneda)

Topic. UNIVERSITY LEARNING IN MEDIEVAL ARCHAEOLOGY

9.00-9.30: H. Anderson, *Teaching Medieval Archaelogy on Internet. Experiences from Lund University.*

9.30-10.00: E. Roesdahl, *Teaching Medieval Archaelogy Regional and/or European. The problem of textbooks.*

10.00-10.30: K. Lind, *The European Artic becoming Medieval.*

10.30-11.00: Coffee-break.

11.00-11.30: I. Ollich, *Research and Teaching in Experimental Archaelogy. L'Esquerda, a project about agriculture, tools and building in Medieval Ages.*

11.30-12.00: R. Francovich, *Un sistema informatico per l'archeologia medievale: dal territorio al manufacto.*

12.30-13.00: Discussion.

13.00-14.00: Lunch.

14.30-16.00: Visit to the Cathedral.

Topic. GENERAL QUESTIONS IN CURRENT RESEARCH

16.30-17.00: G. Mangelsdorf, *The Development of Medieval Archaelogy in East Germany since 1990.*

17.00-17.30: J.L. Bintliff, *Recent Development and New Approaches to the Archaelogy of Medieval Greece.*

17.30-18.00: T. O'Keeffe, *French and Spanish influence on Romanesque Style in England and Ireland. Patterns and Processes of Transmission.*

18.00-19.00: Discussion.

20.30: Dinner.

FRIDAY 1ST OCTOBER
(Excursion in Córdoba. Starting point al Law Faculty at 8.30)

Topic. GENERAL QUESTIONS IN CURRENT RESEARCH

11.00-11.30: J. Décaens, A.M. Flambard, *Méthodologie pour l'étude des châteaux en Normandie.*

11.30-12.00: L. Kajzer, *New Research Problems in Castellology in Central-East Europe.*

12.00-13.30: Visit to the Córdoba Mosque.

14.00-15.00: Lunch.

16.00-18.00: Visit to Madinat a-Zahra.

SATURDAY 2ND OCTOBER
(Fundición Real, Casa de la Moneda)

Topic. SPECIFIC RESEARCH PROJECTS

9.00-9.30: T. Stefanovicova, *The Development and Problems of Medieval Archaelogy on the Middle Danube.*

9.30-10.00: R. Bertelsen, *Fishing Communities of the North, 800-1800. Kholmogory, the nave of Medieval Northwestern Russia.*

10.00-10.30: Cofee break.

11.00-11.30: H. Kócka-Krenz, *Poznan-sedes regni principales at the beginning of Polish Piast State.*

11.30-12.00: T. Barry, J. de Meulemeester and J.M. Poisson, *Research Project of Castle in the Rhône Valley.*

12.00-13.00: Discussion.

13.00-14.00: Lunch.

Topic. MEDIEVAL ARCHAELOGY IN THE IBERIAN PENINSULA

14.30-15.00: A. Gutiérrez, *Visigothic and Early Medieval Christian Archaelogy in Spain (5th-10th centuries).*

15.00-15.30: R. Córdoba, *Late medieval Christian Archaelogy in Spain (11th-15th centuries).*

15.30-16.00: S. Macias, *Bilan d'lArchéologie Médiévale au Portugal.*

16.00-16.30: Coffee-break.

16.30-17.00: F. Valdés, *Islamic Archaelogy in Spain (8th-11th centuries).*

17.00-17.30: M. Valor, *Islamic Archaelogy in Spain (12th-15th centuries).*

17.30-18.30: Discussion.

18.30-19.30: Visit to the Medieval palaces in the Real Alcázar de Sevilla.

21.00: Dinner.

PARTICIPANTS

Andersson, H.
Barry, T.B.
Bertelsen, R.
Bintliff, J.L.
Carmona Ruiz, M.A.
Córdoba La Llave, R.
Décaens, J.
Ericsson, I.
Flambard Héricher, A.M.
Graham-Campbell, J.
Kajzer, L.
Kóčka-Krenz, H.
Lind, K.
Mangelsdorf, G.
Meulemeester, J.
O'Keeffe, T.
Ollich i Castanyer, I.
Poisson, J.M.
Roesdahl, E.
Valdés Fernández, F.
Valor Piechotta, M.

CONTENTS

Se terminó de imprimir este libro en los talleres gráficos
de Pedro Cid, S. A., el día 10 de diciembre de 2001,
festividad de Ntra. Sra. de Loreto,
en Madrid